Nellie Ó Cléirigh

Veronica Rowe

Limerick Lace

A Social History
and
A Maker's Manual

Colin Smythe
Gerrards Cross 1995

First published in 1995 by Colin Smythe Limited
Gerrards Cross, Buckinghamshire.

British Library Cataloguing-in-Publication Data

A catalogue record for this book is available from the British Library.

ISBN 0-86140-368-1

Produced in Great Britain

Contents

Forewords

Much of the material in this book was collected in the mid 1980s because it was intended to be included in the Dolmen Press book on Carrickmacross Lace which was published in 1985. Liam Miller, the publisher, decided that it was better to use the Carrickmacross material on its own so the Limerick research was put away for future use. In the meantime, Veronica Rowe had been sorting the superb material inherited from her grand-mother, Mrs Florence Vere O'Brien. We decided that if we combined our resources we could produce a much better book than if either of us used one set of material.

Apart from the instructions for making Limerick lace, the book contains a great deal of Irish social history, much of which was contributed by nuns who are no longer alive, such as Sister de Lourdes of the Irish Sisters of Charity.

My collection of all the kinds of lace made in Ireland contains more Limerick pieces than any other variety. The beautiful stole of tambour made in the Mercy Convent in Dunmore East, Co. Waterford, was given to my mother as a wedding present in 1925; the ecru stole in darned net was given to Mrs May Hally by the same nuns some years earlier. The large veil or train with the chain stitch in thick thread was bought by me at the auction of the contents of Mulcahy's of Lady's Abbey in Co. Tipperary, in the mid 1970s, as was the cape. Both obviously came from the same school as they feature the outline chain stitch with heavy thread. The very pretty fichu was purchased at an auction in Knightstown, Valentia Island, Co. Kerry. Pieces from the collection have been shown in Dublin and elsewhere in Ireland, at the Edinburgh Festival and in the United States.

I wish to express my thanks to all the people who helped me in the compilation of this book and especially the late Ada Longfield Leask, the sisters of the Good Shepherd Convent, Limerick, the Mercy Convent, Kinsale, the Presentation Convent, Cahirciveen, Pamela Fegan, Maeve Lynam, Anthony and Mary Murphy, Anita Puigcerver-Rumbold, Mrs Beatrice Dixon and the late Freddie Dixon especially for the material about Lady Aberdeen. The staff of the National Library, Dublin, and the Library of the Royal Dublin Society, Dublin were very helpful.

I am very grateful to Essex Record Office for historical material, and to the Royal Dublin Society, who allowed me to reproduce designs from their portfolio of prizewinners.

I want to thank Veronica Rowe for joining with me in this project, and David Rowe for his help in editing.

My special thanks to Cormac for proof-reading and patience.

Nellie Ó Cléirigh

Most of the information on the Limerick Lace School comes from my grandmother, Florence Vere O'Brien's own diaries, letters and articles, as well as her collection of contemporary newspaper cuttings. All these items came to me, along with the remainder of the lace from the Lace School, from my aunt, Flora Vere O'Brien, Florence's younger daughter, who continued to live at the family home, Ballyalla, near Ennis, Co. Clare, until the late 1950s. When Flora moved to a smaller house, she took the lace collection with her, fortunately packed in a metal box, as it was subsequently stored in an outhouse until her death in 1970.

In recent years there has been a revival of interest in the craft of lacemaking, and in the history of an industry, which, at one time, employed many hundreds of women. A number of lace exhibitions have been organised, and a Guild of Irish Lacemakers has been established. One of the most important of the exhibitions was the 'Irish Lace Exhibition' mounted in Dublin to celebrate the city's millennium in 1988, and also to commemorate the centenary of the first competition for lace designs, offered by the Royal Dublin Society in 1888. At the 'Irish Lace Exhibition' the section showing Florence Vere O'Brien's collection generated much interest, and I was encouraged by Dr. Muriel Gahan, one of the main organisers, to do further research into the background of the collection.

I would like to thank all those who helped me with this research, particularly my cousins, Elinor Wiltshire, Susanne O'Brien, Grania Weir and Sylvia Reynolds, for their help in proof reading and in sorting out family relationships. Mairead Dunleavy, formerly curator of the Textile Department of the National Museum (now Director of the Hunt Museum, Limerick), has been most supportive; and I have also received encouragement from Linda Ballard of the Ulster Folk and Transport Museum and from Jane Houston-Almqvist. Dorothy Stewart told me about her great-grandmother, Mrs Mills, who came from Coggeshall in Essex to teach lace design in Limerick in the 1840s. Felicity O'Mahony, of the Manuscript Room in Trinity College, Dublin, was most helpful, as were the librarian and staff of the Royal Dublin Society Library, and of the Limerick College of Art Library. Patricia May helped with photocopying old newspaper cuttings. Judith Badman, Norman Campion, Colin Smythe, Peter Lamb and David Rowe contributed their time and skills in photographing the lace and other items. I must particularly mention George Morrison for his expert work in rephotographing my old photographs.

It has been a great pleasure to work with Nellie Ó Cléirigh on this project.

Finally I must particularly thank my husband David for his unfailing patience and encouragement during the research for this book and for his invaluable work in editing and with word processing.

Veronica Rowe

Part One:
Limerick Lace

Introduction

Limerick is probably the most famous of all Irish laces. When President Kennedy came to Limerick in 1963, the Lord Mayor, the late Mrs Frances Condell, presented him with a Christening Robe of Limerick lace, and other important visitors have also been delighted to receive gifts of this prestigious lace.

The making of the type of lace known as 'Limerick' became possible when machine-made net became readily available. Limerick lace is a form of embroidery on net: being either chain stitch (tambour) or darned net also called run-lace, or a combination of both techniques. Sometimes appliqué was used and even net appliquéd on net, which made a gossamer fabric. Like Carrickmacross lace, which was also a form of embroidery on net, Limerick lace had fillings of run-lace stitches, which were intended to embellish the fabric. Neither Limerick nor Carrickmacross are true laces in the rigidly technical sense of the term, because they are not made entirely 'with the needle'.

When net had to be made by hand it was a very expensive fabric. Various efforts were made on the continent and in England to invent a machine which would make net; some of the earliest efforts at the end of the eighteenth century were based on stocking-making machines. It was not until Heathcoat invented his net-making machine and a factory was set up at Tiverton, Devon, in 1815 that a satisfactory net was produced. Most important for Irish lace makers was the fact that cheap net became readily available, especially after 1823 when Heathcoat's patent expired. The first Irish lace, using machine net as its base, was Carrickmacross, where fine cotton was appliqued on to the net. The making of this lace commenced in 1823 but it was a small undertaking begun by Mrs Grey Porter, the wife of the Church of Ireland rector at Donaghmoyne near Carrickmacross.

Limerick Lace History

The Limerick lace industry was entirely different. It was the first Irish lace-making venture set up on a purely commercial basis. In 1828 Charles Walker, a native of Oxford, brought twenty four girls to Limerick 'skilled in the art of lace embroidery' to teach lace-making. According to an article in *Victorian History of the County of Essex* published in 1907 (Essex Record Office) Charles Walker 'had married a lady who was mistress of an extensive lace manufactory in Essex'. Walker had first set up a lace school in the neighbourhood of Marden Ash, Ongar, where he was living in 1823 and was described in that year as a lace manufacturer. He was stated to be a man of 'literary and artistic tastes and educated for the church, but marrying the daughter of a lace manufacturer, he set up in that business in Essex, working for the London wholesale trade'. According to the same article the making of tambour lace had been brought to the area from France at the beginning of the nineteenth century by a Mr. Drago. He had settled in the Coggeshall area with his daughters and set up a workroom to teach tambour lace. The name 'Coggeshall' seems to have been applied to all lace made in that part of Essex.

At the beginning of this century Jacob Dalton of Coggeshall reported that his mother, who was one of the Frenchman's pupils and for many years carried on a tambour-room of her own, refused a very advantageous offer to go to Ireland. This was a time of recession in the lace industry in southern England which was probably why girls were willing to go to Ireland.

Charles Walker did a short tour of Ireland and examined various districts and localities before choosing Limerick for his lace industry. He was probably attracted by the large population of unemployed females providing cheap labour. Limerick had a thriving glove-making industry in the previous years so there was an existing tradition of factory work. Walker's investment was very substantial, as according to *The Limerick Chronicle* of 4 November 1843 he had expended the sum of £20,000, (modern equivalent about £1,150,000), a very considerable amount at that time, in establishing the lace factory.

The first factory in Limerick was set up in Mount Kennet, on the riverside. According to one account it was 'a large building with spacious rooms and afforded ample accommodation for the workers which at that time numbered about five hundred'.[1] To get a place in the factory was quite difficult. Each girl had to provide a certificate from a doctor as well as one giving her age which was to be between eleven and fourteen years. A reference from some influential citizen had also to be provided. The hours of working were from 6 a.m. to 6 p.m., with the usual breakfast and dinner hours. The several kinds of work then done were fichus, blond lace trimming and grey lace (spotted), traced by tambour workers and filled by runners. The principal teachers were the Misses Mansfield, Curran and Grace.[2]

After about seven or eight years during which the business was carried on at Mount Kennet, Mr. Walker was obliged to give up the store to the landlord who required it for his own use. A factory at Mulgrave Street was then opened and everything went on well until Mr. Walker's death, in 1843. He was succeeded by Mr. Lambert and later by a Mr. Benry or Berry. The last named resided in London and came to Limerick occasionally to look after the business. It appears that Miss Mansfield, who came with Walker, later married a Dr. O'Halloran and was also involved in the running of the business. She was responsible for its further transfer to Glentworth Street. At this period the type of work being made was 'floss work, satin stitch, Valencienne, two-stitch and moss-work' but already the introduction of machine-made lace interfered, especially with 'the running work' and 'caused a great dullness'.

In the early days mention is made of the names of Marianne Hartigan, who 'designed from natural flowers and fruit', and Kate O'Brien who spent the first 2s. 6d. which she earned on a doll.[3]

In his early venture Walker was associated with a Mr. Henning, an exclusive London lace merchant. While this connection lasted, there was a ready market in England for the work made in Limerick; but with Henning's failure in business some years afterwards, the entire responsibility of marketing the product fell to Walker, who opened a London outlet on his own account. He also had Limerick lace taken through England by hawkers.[4]

According to Mrs Palliser in her *History of Lace*, republished in 1984, an early patron was Lady Normanby, wife of the Lord Lieutenant. She gave great encouragement to the fabric, causing dresses to be made, not only for herself but also for Her Majesty, the Queen of the Belgians and the Grand Duchess of Baden.

Walker brought to Limerick another Englishman named Lloyd to help and this man later opened a factory for himself. A third, Leicester Greaves of Cork, also ran a factory in Limerick for some years and was then succeeded by his widow. A Mr M'Clure, a Mr Forrest of Limerick and Dublin, and a partnership of Lambert and Bury were also engaged in the trade as well as various smaller producers, including John Bradley and John Robertson.[5]

The numbers employed were amazingly high. Mr. and Mrs Samuel Hall who toured Ireland in 1838, 1840 and 1853, published an account of their travels in which they left a very vivid description of the lace industry in Limerick. They reported that Walker employed 1,100 females, about 800 of whom were apprentices working in the factories at Limerick and Kilrush; while about 300 were employed at their own homes in the counties of Limerick and Clare. Lambert and Bury, who were in Glentworth Street, employed 700; Forrest in Abbey Court 500; M'Clure in Clare Street 250; Mr. Rolf (of Courtaulds) in Patrick Street or Clare Street, sixty; Mrs Leicester Greaves thirty; these were all first class workers. A further thirty persons employed 300 young females who worked in their own homes. The total of almost 3,000 employees must have added considerably to Limerick's economy. A factory at Kilrush in Co Clare seems to have specialised in design because according to notes left by one of Mrs Vere O'Brien's 'older workers', Ellen Devitt and Mary Moriarty were sent to Kilrush 'to learn designing'.

The Halls recorded that the standard was then so high that the Limerick manufacture not only rivalled, but surpassed, that of any district in England. Walker later offered a large wager that he would select a hundred Irish girls from among his workers, who would produce any given piece of lace superior to any

Limerick Tambour lace child's apron. Collection Limerick Museum. Photo: Limerick Museum.

Left: Tambour lace, 1840. Collection National Museum. Photo: Peter Lamb.

Right: Darned net piece dated 1840. Ó Cléirigh Collection. Photo: Colin Smythe.

similar work made by the same number of girls from France, Flanders, Saxony or Germany.

Mr. Walker's factory produced mainly tambour lace. In the late 1830s Sir Jonas Rolfe – a director of Courtaulds – introduced the making of run lace to Limerick. He invited a lady from Coggeshall, Mrs Mary Mills, to come to Limerick with her husband and two young children, to teach run-lace making in his new factory in Clare Street. Mrs Mills was an experienced designer and had won a gold medal for one of her designs at a South Kensington lace competition. Mr. Mills was also employed in the Courtaulds factory in the capacity of bookkeeper/accountant.[6]

The Halls reported in 1844 that about 1700 females were employed in the various branches of the trade 'consisting of tambourers, runners, darners, menders, washers, finishers, framers, muslin-embroiderers and lace open-workers'. The ages of the workers varied from eight to thirty years. Presumably, after thirty their eye-sight was no longer good enough, though Limerick workers fared better than Brussels lacemakers who often went blind at twenty one.

The social consequences of the lace industry are well described by the Halls: 'The influence of these establishments has been largely felt in Limerick and its vicinity. The cottages of the workers are conspicuous for neatness and order; and very many of the apprentices have sums varying from One Pound to Twenty deposited in the Savings Bank, a considerable number of them earning more than a day labourer and the employment continuing through the whole year.'

Another significant piece of information supplied by the Halls was that Mr. Lloyd annually visited Brussels, Caen and other parts of France to collect new designs, thus being able to produce specimens as elegant and highly-wrought as any continental pieces. Lloyd seems to be the only manufacturer recorded as visiting the Continental lace-making areas.

Some idea of prices at this period and their relative value can be got from Mrs Hall's purchases in Limerick. She bought two lappets for which she paid 8s. 6d. and 7s. respectively and which she considered such value that she would have paid half as much again for inferior articles in London. An elaborate collar in six different stitches and inlaid with the finest cambric cost 10s. as against 16s. in London. Other purchases were a muslin collar made in Co. Clare at 15s., a habit-shirt at 10s., a canezone at 12s. 6d. and a beautiful shawl for £1. 9s., but this last was a wholesale price. Mrs Hall was, of course, buying all these goods at source. Before they reached the English market, many middlemen would have taken their profit as well as the shopkeeper. In fact, at this period, good quality Limerick lace was not considered cheap.

The industry in Limerick continued to prosper, though on their return visit, the Halls could comment that a vast quantity of inferior material was constantly thrown on the market. The standard seems to have fallen in the next few years. There was no attempt to change or improve designs. According to the Essex records Walker sold his Limerick business in 1841 'but his successor becoming bankrupt, he never received the purchase money and died in 1842, his ingenuity and industry ill-rewarded'. The information in the Essex records must be looked at with some scepticism because the date of Walker's death is incorrect. He did not die until November 1843. According to his obituary from *The Limerick Chronicle* of 4 November of that year he had just died! 'He departed this life at his residence at Woodfield, Co. Clare but he had been in declining health for some time past'. The obituary made no mention of the fact that Walker had sold the lace business but listed among his good works that he 'gave to the world a folio volume of a collection of scarce and curious prints of the early masters of the Italian, Greek and Flemish schools illustrative of the history of engraving'. The account in *The Limerick Chronicle* also contained the information that 'there was at that moment (Nov. 1843) in London a native artist who was by him provided with the means to prosacute (*sic*) his studies and cultivate his talents'.

After Walker's death some of his best workers returned to England but we know for certain that large quantities of lace continued to be made in the city, because in the catalogue of the Dublin Exhibition of 1853, fifteen hundred were said to be employed and the firm of Lambert and Bury were quoted as doing 'a large export business'.

The catalogue of the 1853 Exhibition contained some very significant information for the lace trade in listing such exhibits as shawls, scarves, flounces and other garments of machine-made lace where only the edging was finished off by hand. The earlier net-making machines were unable to put any embroidery on the net, giving opportunity to lace makers such as Limerick workers, who could enhance the fabric by hand. But from this time onwards the embroiderers of Limerick, as elsewhere, would have to compete with the machine and therefore be obliged to produce work of very high quality or very cheaply.

Mrs Meredith's book, *The Lace Makers, Sketches of Irish Character* 'with some account of the efforts to establish lacemaking in Ireland' deals with all the kinds of lace made in Ireland when it was published in 1865. Mrs Meredith had no time for Limerick lace which she dismissed as 'having run it's course before crochet began'. It must be admitted however, that this was probably the lowest period in the nineteenth century for Limerick lace. Of interest to English social historians is the fact that Mrs Meredith dedicated her book to Baroness Burdett Coutts, the English philanthropist, who seems to have helped Irish lacemakers, though I have never been able to find out what her exact contribution was.

The catalogue of the 1853 Dublin Exhibition contains a second significant entry: No. 41 from Madame de Beligand, of the Convent of the Good Shepherd, Limerick. She showed ecclesiastical vestments, a Brussels lace veil, and several patterns of Valenciennes lace. All these were bobbin or pillow lace and used a totally different technique from Limerick lace. Madame de Beligand, a native of France, was the second Superior of the Good Shepherd Order in Limerick; she served there from 1848 to 1860 when she went to govern the Order's convent in Aix-la-Chapelle. In Limerick, Madame de Beligand was most anxious to procure a lace teacher so that the 'Penitents', as the unmarried mothers and ex-prostitutes housed at the convent were euphemistically called, could be employed at lighter work than was available in the convent laundry. Arrangements were made through the Order's convents in Belgium, at Namur and Mons; in a short time it was arranged for Amelie van Verevenhaven, an expert in Valencienne lace, to come to the Limerick Convent. The importance of lace-making to Limerick can be judged by the fact that as soon as Mr. Henry O'Shea Q.C. of Limerick heard of the project he kindly offered to defray the travelling expenses of the teacher from Belgium to Limerick. Subsequently, Amelie became a member of the community, and on 27 October 1850 received the religious habit, taking the name of Sister Marie de Ste. Philomene. As recorded in the Convent Annals, she was then aged twenty-five years, and originally came from Saerlurdengen in Belgium. A short time after her reception, she had an unexpected visit from a Belgian Count who had been sent by the Government of her country to interrogate her and, if possible, persuade her to return and thus prevent the industry of Valenciennes lace from being spread outside Belgium. But Sister de Ste. Philomene refused and she lived on in the convent in Limerick until her death on 28 March 1913 and is interred in the nuns cemetery there.[7]

The tradition of lace-making with bobbins was thus set up at the Good Shepherd Convent and continued until the nuns switched to Limerick lace making about 1880.

After the death of Prince Albert in 1861, (when the Court went into deep mourning) and the consequent decline in lace making, Courtaulds left Limerick, but their designer Mrs Honora O'Halloran who ultimately succeeded Mrs Mills, continued the business until it was eventually taken over by Cannocks. Cannocks, Todds, and the Good Shepherd Convent appear to have been the only organised manufacturers of lace in Limerick in the 1870s.

In the early 1880s there was a big revival in the making of Limerick lace partly because the Good Shepherd Nuns had switched to making it, but mainly due to the efforts of Mrs Robert Vere O'Brien. Her contribution is so important that it merits a separate account which has been written by her grand-daughter, Mrs Veronica Rowe. Many of the beautiful designs reproduced in this book are from Mrs Rowe's collection, handed down to her from her grandmother. Perhaps the most important contribution to lace made by Mrs Vere O'Brien was the setting-up of a lace-training school in Limerick in 1893. Mrs Vere O'Brien was also associated with the Convent of Mercy in Kinsale, where she had a stitch named after her: surely the highest tribute that could be paid to any designer.

One factor which led to the revival of lacemaking in Ireland at this period was the realisation that good design was absolutely necessary. In his Report of the Cork Industrial Exhibition, 1883, W. K. Sullivan, President of Queen's College, Cork, wrote 'It is only well designed and finely executed lace that can hold its ground against machine lace. It is consequently of vital importance that Irish lace-workers should work only good designs and meet the uniformity of the machine by the variety of the hand.' Some of the examples at the exhibition were 'well designed and nearly all finely executed, yet in too many the beautiful work was thrown away upon a wretched meaningless design.' W. K. Sullivan elaborated 'This want of design in the lace exhibited and the importance of this kind of work to the south of Ireland, suggested to the Executive Committee the desirability of doing something for this beautiful industry. Among the projects of the Committee was the organization of a series of lectures on industrial topics; it was proposed to build a special lecture room and invite distinguished persons to deliver one or more lectures on some subject upon which they were authorities'. This project fell through but a few lectures were given in the Exhibition building itself and among them two on lace, by Mr. Alan Cole, of the Department of Science and Art in South Kensington, 'an enthusiastic admirer of and a very high authority on everything concerning the art of ornamental needlework 'to quote Dr. Sullivan again. The lectures were illustrated by patterns, photographs, and pieces of real lace. Later Mr. Cole, accompanied by Mr. J. Brenan, R.H.A.. Master of the Cork School of Art and a member of the Executive Committee, made a tour among the convents and schools in the Counties of Cork and Kerry which were centres of the lace industry, gave instruction and advice and exhibited his collection of drawings and samples of lace. This tour was so successful that it was arranged for Mr. Brenan to pay periodical visits to the convents and other centres of the lace industry, thus extending the benefits of the Cork School of Art to the south and west of the country. £200 from the surplus of the Cork Exhibition in 1883 was set aside together with a further £200 from the Department of Science and Art, to procure for the newly formed Crawford school of Art in Cork a very beautiful and instructive collection of samples of lace.[8] A 'Private Committee'was formed in 1884 to improve the design of all the seven kinds of Irish lace listed by them. Several of the Dukes, Duchesses, Earls and Marchionesses on this Committee appear on every charitable organization of this period but most had some connection with the lace or embroidery industries. Miss Keane of Cappoquin came from a family involved in lacemaking before 1837; the Bagwells of Clonmel had set up a coloured embroidery industry at Marlfield; Mrs Arthur Kavanagh's family in Borris, Co. Carlow, were responsible for a tape-lace industry and Mr Robert Vere O'Brien was also a member.[9]

The most important, most famous and certainly the most influential member of the 'Private Committee' set up to improve design, was the Countess of Aberdeen, wife of the Viceroy, the king's representative in Ireland under Gladstone's government. The uncharitable maintained that Lady Aberdeen was the real Viceroy! She was involved in health improvement movements and set up the Women's National Health Association, the Baby Clubs, the children's playgrounds, the pasteurised milk depots, and the early sanatoria, as well as promoting the manufacture of lace and linen.[10]

Lady Aberdeen,
Marchioness of
Aberdeen and Temair.
Postcard,
Ó Cléirigh Collection.

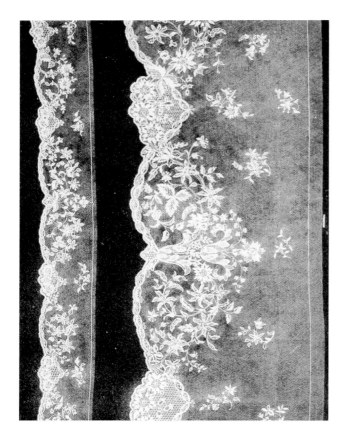

The Aberdeens were in Ireland for only six months in 1886 before having to retire from office on the fall of Gladstone's government. The Marquis of Aberdeen was appointed Governor of Canada and did not return to Ireland until 1906. Lady Aberdeen, however, kept her connections with Ireland and acccording to the Annals of the Convent of Mercy in Kinsale she visited the Lace School there in 1893 and for a longer period in 1894. 'She seemed very interested in the work and through her efforts the school is indebted for a large increase in orders by which we are able to keep about fifty girls constantly employed.'

Funds for the 'Private Committee' to improve design came from a variety of sources, some outside the country. The Skinners Company, Messrs Marshall and Snelgrove, Baroness de Rothschild and Edward Guinness were among the more famous sponsors. The committee proposed to improve design by offering money prizes for the production of designs for the various classes of lace work, including Limerick. They proposed to select, with the advice of recognised authorities, a dozen or more suitable patterns; to order, with a guarantee of payment to the workers, specimens of such patterns executed by picked workers in various districts; to exhibit these specimens in some public institutions in London, Dublin, Belfast, Cork and elsewhere; to make photographs of these specimens for circulation to subscribers to the fund and to dealers in lace. The pattern of the Limerick tambour flounce designed by Miss Emily Anderson, of the Crawford Municipal School of Art, Cork, and made by workers under the supervision of Mrs Vere O'Brien, dates from this period, as do the Limerick lace borders. Of particular interest is the Limerick lace flounce and border which was made at the Convent of Mercy, Kinsale. This design, also by Emily Anderson, was selected by Queen Victoria in 1886.[11] The Queen was a great lace patron and was reputed to like her knickers trimmed with only the best!

The flounce and border of tambour were designed by a nun at the Convent of the Poor Clares, Kenmare, and were made under the direction of Mrs R. Vere O'Brien, of Limerick. Kenmare is best known for its needlepoint lace, but other varieties were made there.

Left: Limerick lace flounce and border. Design by Miss Emily Anderson of the Crawford School of Art, Cork. Selected by Queen Victoria in 1886. Photo from *A Renascence of the Irish Art of Lace Making*, by Alan Cole, 1888.

Right: Flounce and border in Limerick tambour designed by a nun of the Poor Clares Convent Kenmare. Made by workers under the direction of Mrs. R. Vere O'Brien of Limerick. Photo same source as above.

Working Conditions and Pay

In Walker's time (1840s) it is reported that the children trained for seven years, and girls worked on calico for three to six months: presumably this was a period of training. Conditions must have been rather crowded: 300 girls were reported to work in the room under a Mrs Blake. Women were quoted as earning as much as 15s. to 20s. per week by working until 12.00 at night (in 1847, at the height of the Famine). Lace skirts, and sprigged net for bodices, were made by two sets of workers, one lot outlining and the other darning. These were all washed and slightly stiffened.[12]

In their tours taken in 1838 and 1840, the Halls noted 'The utmost attention is paid to the social and moral condition of the workers; and good habits are studiously taught them as well as their business; they are remarkably clean and well ordered; and their appearance is healthy and comfortable. Their health is carefully watched by medical practitioners, who attend upon them in their houses in cases of illness, the expense of which is defrayed by the masters.'

Other Centres of Limerick Lace

Like other Irish laces, the making of 'Limerick' spread outside the area where it had originated and from which it got its name.

Kinsale

One of the earliest centres, outside Limerick itself, was Kinsale, Co. Cork. In 1847, the year of the Great Famine, 'looms were introduced into Kinsale Convent for the manufacture of lace and muslin embroidery' to quote from the annals of the Convent of Mercy. Rev. Mother Francis Bridgman procured the services of an experienced lace-maker from Limerick, and the Board of National Education sent a qualified teacher to teach the embroidery. In 1848, an 'Industrial School' was opened in which employment in various kinds of needlework commenced. The girls who were to learn the lace-making were 'bound' as apprentices for three years, with their parents' consent. This is the only reference I have found to Irish lacemakers being indentured servants. The Annals of Kinsale Convent also include the information that community funds were made available to provide the necessary materials. Kinsale was an area where there was great poverty and any paid work was welcomed. At the 1853 Exhibition in Dublin the nuns showed Irish point lace, crochet, Limerick lace, Honiton lace, embroidery in silk and gold, feather and muslin flowers and satin stitch embroidery.

According to the Department of Technical Instruction Report for 1902, in the early days of lace making in Kinsale no drawing was taught. For about three months the young learners were compelled to 'stab a needle through a piece of calico on which the pattern had been traced.' Presumably, this would give them some sense of outline but would not replace practice in drawing.

In 1885 the Kinsale lace school was brought into association with the South Kensington Establishment, the prestigous School of Art in London. This was the period when the school was involved with Mr James Brenan and Alan Cole from the Department of Science and Art in London, and with Lady Aberdeen, the wife of the Viceroy. It was also when the standard of design and workmanship was highest at Kinsale. Scholarships were obtained by the school in three succeeding years, two of the winners being Cecilia Keyes in 1892 and Albinia Collins. Cecilia Keyes eventually returned to the Kinsale convent and became a well-known designer, specialising in the flowers of the district. There is a tradition in Kinsale that she had drawn every flower in the area. Cecilia had been brought up in the convent in Kinsale and may have been an orphan or illegitimate. The chance to attend a London School of Art was a great achievement for these girls but their life on scholarships must have been lonely and spartan. In addition Cecilia Keyes was

Handkerchief designed by Cecilia Keyes of the Branch School of Art, Convent of Mercy, Kinsale. Royal Dublin Society album. ref. 84654. 1899.

handicapped by being lame.[13]

The Convent in Kinsale was regarded as a good training school in 1901. A letter from Emily Anderson, an advisor on lace-making employed by the Department of Agriculture and Technical Instruction, to Mrs Vere O'Brien, discusses the advisability of sending a girl to train at the Art Class in Kinsale or at the School of Art in Dublin. The letter writer considered that 'Kinsale excells in Limerick'.[14]

As many as 140 girls were employed in Kinsale in 1909 but the number varied according to the demand.

The annals of the Mercy Convent in Kinsale record, too, that in addition to Limerick, the girls produced Greek lace and altar cloths, albs and a 'good many other descriptions of delicate needlework'. When the bottom fell out of the lace market during World War 1 the nuns purchased knitting-machines to make stockings in an attempt to provide employment. The making of habits for the dead, and shirt-making for the military were other business efforts. Today, very little

Workroom of St. Joseph's Convent, Kinsale; about 1900. The frames used by the girls and some finished work are clearly shown. Photo: Souvenir Album presented to the Marquis & Marchioness of Aberdeen and Temair. Ó Cléirigh Collection.

Stole in tambour made at the Mercy Convent, Dunmore East, Co. Waterford, early 20th century. Ó Cléirigh Collection. Photo: National College of Art and Design. (N.C.A.D.).

Right: Enlargement of edging. Photo: N.C.A.D.

credit is given to the religious orders for their varied attempts to combat poverty in Ireland in the nineteenth century.

Dunmore East

The high quality of work made outside Limerick is shown in the stoles made at the Mercy Convent, Dunmore East, Co. Waterford, illustrated here. As well as the tambour (chain-stitch) technique of the stole, excellent darned net was also made there, as shown in the ecru stole illustrated above. It is interesting to speculate where the Dunmore East nuns got their designs, but unfortunately there are no surviving records at the convent. James Brenan, who later became Head of the College of Art in Cork and eventually Dublin, had served in the College in

Waterford earlier. Perhaps he may have procured such good designs for the nuns.

At the 'Ui Breasail Exhibition' in Dublin in 1911, the Dunmore East and Waterford Convents of Mercy specialised in Limerick lace, also 'artificial flowers, collars, handkerchiefs and scarfs'.

The Lace School in Dunmore East did not survive World War I but unsold garments were given as wedding presents to the sisters of the nuns there and at the convent in Philip Street, Waterford, which was founded from Dunmore East. A tambour stole or scarf was presented to the author's mother in 1925.

Left: Darned net ecru stole made at Mercy Convent, Dunmore East, Co. Waterford, early 20th century. Owned by Mrs Mary Murphy, Clonmel. Photo: N.C.A.D.

Right: Enlargement of edging. Photo: N.C.A.D.

Benada Abbey

A large and long-lasting centre existed at Benada Abbey in Sligo where the Irish Sisters of Charity set up a school using a grant from the Congested Districts Board. Sister Mary Lourdes, who was then very elderly, told me in 1978 that when she

Group of lace makers at Irish Sisters of Charity Convent, Benada Abbey, Co. Sligo. Ó Cléirigh Collection.

worked in Benada in 1935 there were still twenty workers in the lace-room. They were well trained in the necessary stitches, one girl, Mary Millar, having been sent by the nuns to train at the School of Art in Kildare Street, Dublin. The workers were paid piece rates. Sister Lourdes did not know what they received but they seemed satisfied enough with it at the time. Rev. Mother was usually in charge of the finances but the money was paid out by the sister in charge of the workroom. Each girl had a pass book to record her earnings. All the patterns came from The School of Art in Kildare Street and were all old designs. The picture above shows the girls in Benada in 1907. Their frames to hold their work are clearly visible in the front row. According to Sister Lourdes much of the work in Benada was sold to Clery's in Dublin. Orders for Church vestments came mainly from Australia and from Irish priests whose families often presented them with a set of vestments on ordination.

Cahirciveen

Another smaller school was at the Presentation Convent in Cahirciveen. There, according to the convent annals a small knitting industry was set up after the Famine (1846-7) to help the poor starving children . Some years later a lady named Eileen McCarthy from Chermong, near Cahirciveen, and known as Madame McCarthy because she had been to France, taught the nuns how to make lace. Unfortunately, the annals do not tell us what kind of lace was made at that time. In 1896, Madame McCarthy came to live in the convent. She gave the sisters money to build a room for the lace making. A reference is made in the annals to 'Limerick lace and a little Carrickmacross' being taught in 'Madame's room'. She died in 1902 and is buried in the convent cemetery. With Mother Clare as her assistant, the lace industry flourished and was marketed in England, France, U.S.A. and in Ireland. Unfortunately, no record survives of the wages paid or the total value of the sales. At the Cahirciveen Feis in June 1905 the exhibits included knitwear and lace from the school. Mother Clare was then in charge of the lace school and two sisters, Sister Joseph and Sister Benignus were sent to the School of Art in Cork to learn Limerick, Carrickmacross and crochet so 'as to be able to assist Mother Clare in teaching lace-making to the girls'. In the following years fewer girls came to 'the factory' as the lace school was called locally. Debbie Casey worked alone at it until

23

her death in 1940. She enjoyed the nickname of 'Debby flounce'.[15]

The main orders for lace to the Cahirciveen convent came from priests and nuns for albs, surplices and altar falls.

Kenmare and Youghal

Sometimes Limerick lace was made in centres which were famous for other varieties. Kenmare and Youghal convents were renowned for their needlepoint but in both areas Limerick as well as high quality crochet were made. Fanny Taylor in her book *Irish Homes and Hearts*, published in 1867, left a horrific description of Kenmare at that period. 'There was no resident landlord and terrible poverty. The building of the church and convent gave employment to very many for some years but the distress has been great since they were completed. The Sisters opened an industrial school which gives employment to several hundreds and here needle-work of all kinds and lace making are carried on; Limerick lace and Irish point and guipure, with many other varieties, are beautifully executed. The great market for the disposal of the lace is in the tourist season, when Kenmare is the halting place between Killarney and Glengarriff. The lace is displayed at the Hotel when the tourists stop to dine, and some who stay longer pay a visit to the convent and see the good effected. Many ladies have been so struck by the sight that they have endeavoured on their return to England to get orders for the lace there, having taken specimens with them to show their friends. Poor children were taught by the nuns and also clothed and fed. I was much struck'.

A later visitor to Kenmare was Susan B. Anthony, an American Quaker in 1883. At that period thirty girls were at work on beautiful Irish point and Limerick lace.

Congested Districts Board

The Congested Districts Board, set up by the British Government in 1891 to improve conditions in the west of Ireland, was responsible for the spread of Limerick lace making to very remote areas. It is not possible to estimate how much of the total lace was made in the Limerick style, but the industry as a whole was very important to the economy. It was claimed that 'there are families in Mayo and Galway which had never possessed a cow until the younger members began to attend the lace classes and by their intelligence and industry became able to add from ten to fifteen shillings per week to the family income'. Very often the money saved was used to pay passages to America.[16]

Lace Co-operatives

Lace Co-operatives to market the product date from the early 1890s but according to an article signed H. Norman, on the 'Irish Agricultural Organisation Society and the Co-operative Movement' in *Leabhar na h-Eireann 1909*, 'the application of the co-operative principle to the marketing of lace has been less successful than to farm produce, the industry being one in which divergency of method and individual initiative often counts for much in dealing with the preparation and disposal of the product'. The sales from Lace Co-operatives were shown in the 1902 Report of the Department of Agriculture and Technical Instruction as

1895	£4,230
1896	£5,227
1897	£6,904
1898	£7,937
1899	£11,130
1900	£23,149

Convent of Mercy,
Killarney.

The Lace Rooms and Schools, Convent of Mercy, Killarney.

Various Centres

The following extract from the Royal Dublin Society *Catalogue of the Art Industries Exhibition* in August 1903 shows the variety of places where Limerick Lace (Tambour and Run) was then made.

St. Joseph's, Kinsale.
St. Vincent's, Cork.
Convent of Mercy, Gort.
Convent of Mercy, Queenstown. (Cobh).
Convent of Mercy, Killarney.
St. Lelia's School, Limerick.
Crawford Municipal Technical Institute, Cork.
Mrs Vere O'Brien's Limerick Lace School.*
Longfield Lace Centre, Cashel.
Longford Lace Industry.
Sisters of Charity, Benada Abbey, Sligo.
Catholic Institution, St. Mary's Cabra, Dublin.
South Presentation Convent, Cork.

1st Prize for a Bridal Veil

Convent of Mercy,
Bantry.

Convent of Mercy, Bantry.

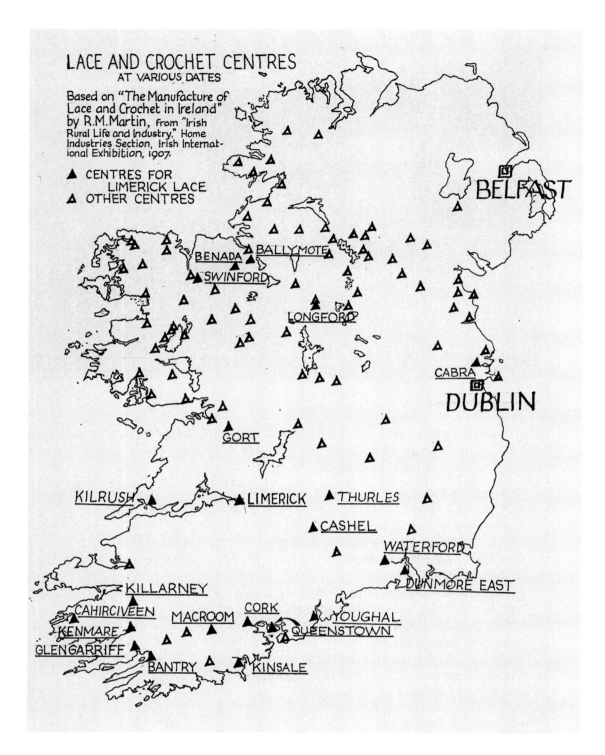

LACE AND CROCHET CENTRES
AT VARIOUS DATES

Based on "The Manufacture of
Lace and Crochet in Ireland"
by R.M.Martin, from "Irish
Rural Life and Industry," Home
Industries Section, Irish Internat-
ional Exhibition, 1907.

▲ CENTRES FOR
      LIMERICK LACE
△ OTHER CENTRES

BELFAST

BENADA   BALLYMOTE
SWINFORD

LONGFORD

CABRA

DUBLIN

GORT

KILRUSH   LIMERICK   THURLES

CASHEL

WATERFORD

KILLARNEY   DUNMORE EAST

CAHIRCIVEEN   MACROOM   CORK   YOUGHAL
KENMARE   QUEENSTOWN
GLENGARRIFF
         BANTRY   KINSALE

Patterns and Designs

The scarcity of patterns and designs is continually mentioned in the surviving
records as well as the fact that the lace makers did not learn drawing. There were
Schools of Art in Ireland but they were very remote from some of the centres of
lace-making.

In Dublin, the Metropolitan School of Art had been founded by the Dublin
Society (later the Royal Dublin Society) in 1731 to 'Improve Husbandry, manufactures and other useful arts and sciences'. In 1849 a school of design was set up
under the Board of Trade. Eventually in 1900 the school came under the control of
the new Department of Agriculture and Technical Instruction for Ireland.[17] Many
good designers were trained in the school at the end of the last century, some of
whose designs are included in this book. The school also sold designs to

Fichu in tambour. Note that design on frill is scaled down version of the main piece. The frill may have been added later as it is in a different net from the triangular main piece. Ó Cléirigh Collection. Photo: the late F. E. Dixon.

Narrow stole or fascinator in darned net. Ó Cléirigh Collection. Photo: P. Lamb.

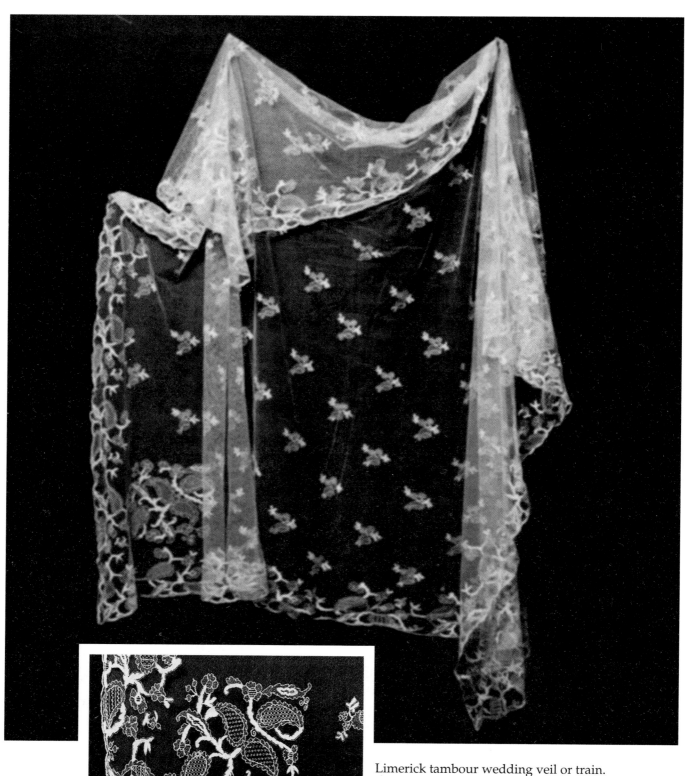

Limerick tambour wedding veil or train.
Ó Cléirigh Collection. Photo: N.C.A.D.

Enlargement showing use of thick thread
which spared the worker from doing several
parallel lines of stitching. Photo: N.C.A.D.

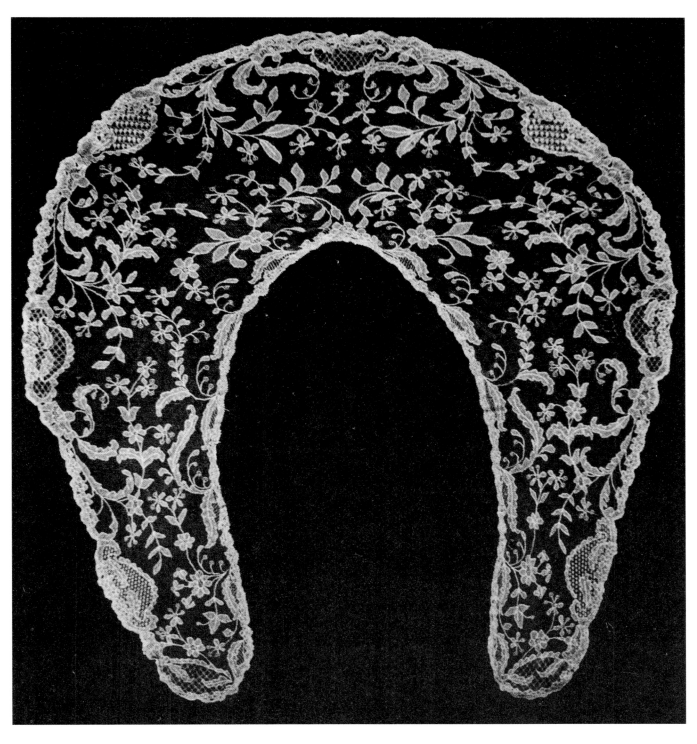

Collar in darned net. Owned by Anita Puigcerver-Rumbold.
Photo: Colin Smythe.

Design No. 404 for darned Limerick lace by Miss Jeanie Tobin, Durrus, Bantry, Co. Cork, taken from the Royal Dublin Society book of designs for lace dated August 1899: entries for one of their competitions.

lacemakers for a small fee.

The Royal Dublin Society's annual competitions were of great importance to all the crafts. From 1888 prizes were awarded for lace designs. Some of the prize-winning designs are included in this book.

In Cork, a School of Art and Design in the late eighteenth century was part of the Royal Cork Institution. The school fell into difficulties but in 1877 an Improved School was established which later became the Crawford School. Its considerable involvement with lace design is well chronicled.[18] In April 1900 during the visit of Queen Victoria to Dublin, specimens of the needlework executed at the Cork School were submitted 'to her Majesty, who was graciously pleased to order 2 embroidered coverlets, which were completed and forwarded to Buckingham Palace.'

There was also a School of Design in Belfast but it closed in 1854. Between 1870 and 1901 a Government School of Art operated there, but both of these were very remote from Limerick lacemakers who were mostly located in the south of Ireland. The School of Art in Limerick was founded in 1852, but did not set up classes in lace design until the early 1900s, then under the auspices of the new Department of Agriculture and Technical Instruction.

At the end of the last century the Arts and Crafts Society of Ireland also contributed to the growth of lace industries. The Society's report for 1894 showed designs by some of the well-known designers such as E. Perry, E. Anderson and Alice Jacob. Others included were W.N.M. Orpen, presumably one of the family of talented painters, and Miss Smithwick and the Countess of Mayo who, with her husband, was responsible for setting up the Arts and Crafts Society in Ireland.

Because Limerick was only one of the various kinds of Irish lace it is not possible to separate its importance to the economy in the last century but it provided paid employment for women who would have had no alternative earnings. Lace makers were described as being the only support of their families, and of being

30

Design No. 445 by Eleanor Rossiter, 4 Tempé Terrace, Dalkey. From R.D.S. book of 1899.

Design No. 446 by Elizabeth Doyle, Tourville, Rathmines Rd., Dublin. From R.D.S. book of 1899.

able to take their parents out of the workhouse. Like any industry it suffered from problems of supply and demand, but lack of suitable patterns and the fact that drawing was not taught were very important factors in the middle years of the last century. Ireland had no 'ateliers' or design studios which were a normal part of lace industries in France and Belgium. Especially when much of the work was centered in convents the nuns were very remote from the world of fashion.

The convents had one very important point in their favour. They provided much better continuity than small undertakings set up by individuals.

Front view of Royal Irish Industries depot in Grafton St., Dublin. From Souvenir Album presented to the Marquis and Marchioness of Aberdeen and Temair. Photo: the late F.E. Dixon.

Advertisement for depot opposite. Ó Cléirigh Collection.

Interior of the Irish Industries depot. From same source as above.

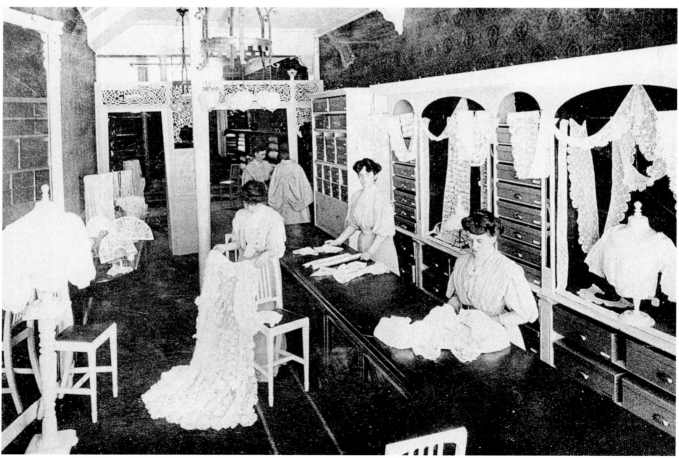

Some of Clery's workers of handmade Irish lace. Postcard: date unknown, but marked on back "Real Photo". Ó Cléirigh Collection.

Sales Outlets

Shops

In the early years of Limerick lace making, the sales were arranged by the owners of the factories, such as Walker and Lloyd. As the industry declined in the middle of the last century retail shops in Limerick, Cork, Dublin and London were the usual outlets. These varied from 'Lace Shops' to department stores. In the Dublin Exhibition of 1853 the principal shops were quoted as 'Atkinsons, Fry, Coulson of Lisburn, and James Forrest and Son who had shops both in Limerick and Dublin.' One of the most important outlets was the Irish Lace Depot in Grafton St., Dublin started by Ben Lindsey, a lace dealer. On his death the business was bought by Lady Aberdeen, who set up a voluntary committee to run it. The depot supplied patterns and designs as well as disposing of the lace. Picture on the facing page shows the interior of the Dublin shop. Another major outlet was Walpoles, who specialised in linen.

The Hibernian Lace Co., 53 Lower Sackville St. (now O'Connell St.) in Dublin claimed early this century that they were 'Manufacturers of all classes of Irish Handmade Lace.'

In 1894 the Irish Lace and Art Bureau at 17 Nassau St., Dublin advertised in the *New Ireland Review* that 'Tourists and visitors to Dublin are respectfully solicited to visit our show rooms where numerous specimens of the famous laces of Ireland may be inspected: Youghal, New Ross, Kenmare, Clones, Kinsale, Innishmacsaint, Limerick etc. Lace and embroidery for church purposes a speciality'. In the same book, Brown Thomas of Grafton St. and Duke Street advertised Irish lace and said that they were 'two minutes from the Shelbourne Hotel'. The firm of Pims, like Walpoles no longer with us, advertised table linens and Irish laces. They were at pains to show reproductions of the medals won by them at various exhibitions but there was no information to show what the medals were for.

Robinson Cleavers in Belfast advertised 'British and foreign lace' but specified that 'every description of Irish lace could be made to order'. Unusually, they offered patterns or rubbings of designs post free.

Royal Irish Industries depot, London: from programme Manchester Exhibition, 1907. Rowe Collection.

Atkinson showcase, early 20th century. Photo: the late F.E. Dixon.

34

The major Department stores such as Switzers, Brown Thomas, and Arnotts in Dublin all sold Irish lace. Clerys in O'Connell Street must have had their own lace-makers if we are to judge from the post card at page 34.

The Irish Industries Association opened a shop in London in 1891. The illustration at page 34 shows it to have been quite an impressive establishment. According to an article in September of that year in *The Lady of the House* the shop at 20 Motcombe Street was 'in a quiet little thoroughfare in the heart of Belgravia' and was in pretty colouring, 'light green on the facia board'. The Manageress was a Wexford woman, Miss Keating.

Another London outlet was the Irish Work Society at 233 Regent Street. H. Goblet of Milk Street, Copestake, Moore, Crampton and Co. and Haywards were all selling Irish lace in London and showed their wares as early as the 1862 International Exhibition there.

Possibly the last surviving lace shop was at Mary Street in Dublin run by a Mrs Gorman, which lasted up to the 1950s.

Exhibitions

Another major outlet for lace was through exhibitions. The Crystal Palace Exhibition in London in 1851 showed 'Lacework of Limerick held in high estimation'. After the Crystal Palace and the great Paris Exhibitions most major cities in Europe and later in America held exhibitions.

Even during the Great Famine an exhibition was held in Dublin in 1847, where lace was displayed by Messrs Atkinsons, Fry, Coulsons of Lisburn, and Messrs Forrest and Sons. The Ladies Industrial Society received 'a warm enconium both for the neatness of the goods exhibited by them and the praiseworthy object sought to be attained in elevating the industrial character of the female poor'.

The first Irish exhibition with a large display of Irish lace was in Dublin in 1853. The report of the exhibition included the following information 'Manufacture of lace had recently been extended to almost the whole country. Exhibits were superior to those exhibited at any previous exhibition'. 1,500 women were stated to be employed in the city of Limerick. The wide variety of garments made from Limerick lace is shown in the entry of Messrs Lambert and Bury, Designers and Manufacturers 'Half squares, berthes, jackets, handkerchiefs, scarfs, falls, chemisettes, and collars'.

A medal won at any of these exhibitions would ensure a flow of orders and a purchase by a royal patron was even more important.

Lace workers at Vice-Regal Lodge. Photo from Souvenir Album presented to the Marquis and Marchioness of Aberdeen and Temair.

Arnott & Co. DUBLIN, ...IRELAND

SILK MERCERS, WAREHOUSEMEN, DRAPERS, ETC.,

Desire to inform visitors to this Exhibition and those who intend going to Ireland, that they have for the past fifty-one years been engaged in selling Irish Manufactures, and that they hold at present a magnificent stock of Irish Industries, including the following:

POPLINS, LACES, AND LACE HANDKERCHIEFS;

BALBRIGGAN HOSE;

BLARNEY, DONEGAL, ATHLONE, AND LUCAN TWEEDS AND SERGES;

BALLINAKEL FLANNELS, BLANKETS, AND RUGS;

BELFAST LINENS, SHIRTS, COLLARS, AND SKIRTINGS;

DRAWING-ROOM, DINING-ROOM, AND BED-ROOM FURNITURE;

SILK HANDKERCHIEFS, HATS, SHOES, ETC.

DUBLIN, ...IRELAND Arnott & Co.

Arnott & Co. advertisement from catalogue of Chicago Exhibition.

An International Exhibition in 1862 mentioned 'the undoubted aptitude for lace-making of the women of Ireland' in its jurors' report.

The Irish Exhibition of Arts and Manufactures held in the grounds of the Rotunda Hospital in Dublin in 1882 had eighteen lace entries; no type was specified but entries came from the Good Shepherd Convent in Limerick. Medals were won by Todd Burns, Dublin, Cannock and Co. Limerick, Dwyer and Co., Cork and Pat Keelan in Carrickmacross.

The Chicago Fair of 1893, officially titled 'The World Colombian Exposition', was a major outlet for Irish lace. The Irish presence there was the brain-child of Lady Aberdeen, who was living in Canada at the time, but made several visits to Ireland to arrange, in conjunction with the Irish Industries Association, the 'Irish village' at the Exposition. Lady Aberdeen visited Limerick with Mr. Peter White who was to manage the Irish entry. After a civic reception she lunched at the Palace, the residence of the Church of Ireland Bishop, Dr. Graves, where she received a number of old and genuine Limerick lace makers, who were then employed by

Mrs Vere O'Brien 'who has done so much for Limerick lace'. One of the workers said she was eighty-six years of age and was the sole survivor of the four women who worked the bridal veil for Queen Victoria.

On one of her Irish visits Lady Aberdeen personally chose forty girls who went to demonstrate various crafts at the Fair, including lace making, and they were also to sell the Irish products. Lady Aberdeen actually guaranteed the girls safety to their mothers! It must have been a marvellous experience for the girls but none of them appear to have left any written account of it.

Lady Aberdeen used her connections to get people like Cardinal Gibbons and Gordon Selfridge to help. The latter ordered a vest and a wedding veil. He was then a director of Marshal Field in Chicago – this was before he opened Selfridges in London. He undertook to provide wax models and glass cases for the exhibition. We must also give Lady Aberdeen credit for some quick thinking. When she discovered that President Cleveland would not be visiting the Irish Village after the opening of the Fair, she rushed six of the Irish girls (the prettiest ones) to the railway station to give a blackthorn stick and a Limerick lace handkerchief to the departing President.

The Irish Village was one of the few financially successful exhibits and netted £50,000 for the workers of Ireland and a further sum of £5,000, part of which was used to finance an Irish Depot in Chicago. Lord Aberdeen guaranteed the salary of the manager and helped to raise money for the setting up of the village. The success of the Irish exhibit was to be specially admired as the manager, Peter White, died suddenly and his work was completed by his wife.

The catalogue of the Chicago exhibition gives the names of some of the lace makers like Ellen Murphy who 'shows how the pretty light Limerick lace is made, which is regaining its popularity since Mrs Vere O'Brien and other ladies and gentlemen have set to work to improve the designs'. Some of those who ran the industries must also have gone to work at the Fair because Miss Mayne, Miss Robinson and Miss Keane (presumably of the Cappoquin school) showed 'all manner of cottage industries and not only lace and embroideries of many kinds, but hosiery and underclothing, woollens and baskets from Letterfrack and we know not what else'.[19]

The Ballymaclinton Exhibition in London in 1908 included working lace-makers. The 'colleen' wearing a cloak in the picture shown here was a Miss Simpson. The Irish Lace School earned silver and bronze medals. According to the

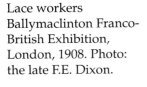

Lace workers Ballymaclinton Franco-British Exhibition, London, 1908. Photo: the late F.E. Dixon.

Children from St. Ann's Industrial School Booterstown, Co. Dublin, at the Ui Breasail Exhibition, Ballsbridge, Dublin, 1911. Photo from *Slainte*, the journal of the Women's National Health Association of Ireland. Ó Cléirigh Collection.

catalogue of the Exhibition, Queen Alexander, considered as an expert needlewoman, was fascinated with the lace exhibits which were shown as examples of work from the convents of Belturbet, Ardee, Dalkey and Youghal, to name but a few'. Probably the last major contribution to the lace industry made by Lady Aberdeen was the Ui Breasail Exhibition inBallsbridge 1911. *Slainte* ("Health") was the journal of the Womens National Health Association of Ireland set up by Lady Aberdeen and she used the name "Ui Breasail" ("Isle of the Blessed") for the huge exhibition held in Ballsbridge. The scope of the exhibits can be seen from the list of the firms participating but also included were 'Cottage and Artisan Cookery, Home Preservation of Fruits, Irish cheese, the Pasteurised Milk Depot, the Babies Club Exhibit, How to clean a house, Dress Cutting made Easy, the Travelling Health Caravan and a goat show', to name only a selection. Entertainments included Tea Gardens, a Cafe Chantant, Choir, A Concert Party, Pageants, Village Hall Entertainments, a Bird Circus, bands and pipers.

Of more interest to lace makers were entries like that of James Kirby and Co., 20 George's Street, Limerick who had 'a fine show of Irish lace of all kinds', and Miss K. A. Bullen of 4 Georges Quay, Cork who showed that 'the art of lace-making has been brought to a fine art in the rebel city.' Miss Bullen found this the most successful exhibition she ever showed at. Miss N. Dunne was the 'courteous manager of Mrs Vere O'Brien's Limerick Lace School' at a stall where 'the lace itself was its own recommendation, for it would have been impossible to get together a more exquisite collection than was shown here'.

What was unusual about the Ui Breasail Exhibition was the display of lace and other goods made at Irish Industrial Schools. There were sixty-six such schools in Ireland in 1911 of which forty-four were for girls – forty-one for Catholic girls and three for Protestants – a total of 4,410 girls. The displays given by the girls included lace making and embroidery. The picture shows girls from St. Ann's Industrial School, Booterstown, Dublin.[20]

Economic and Social Factors

Much lace was made in convents which were far removed from centres of fashion. In Kinsale there must have been some effort to keep up with changes in design as a number of fashion magazines from the period are on display in the local Museum.

Irish workers were also competing with European lace makers. Particularly in Belgium and Switzerland there was a huge labour force involved in lace-making and the market became oversupplied.

The situation was helped somewhat after 1870, because during the Franco-Prussian War, additional markets were opened up in America, north and south, as well as in England, to Irish goods. All Irish laces would have had improved markets but it is not possible to say how much of the extra trade went to Limerick.

Royal visits were a great boost to the lace industry in Ireland. In July 1911 the royal visit of King Edward Vll and Queen Alexandra included a dinner at Dublin Castle on the night of their arrival, a levee two days later, a visit to Leopardstown Races and a state banquet that evening, followed by a chapter of the Most Illustrious Order of St. Patrick. On Tuesday July 11th there was a garden party in the grounds of the Viceregal Lodge, now Aras an Uachtaráin, and that night their Majesties held a court at Dublin Castle. The picture of the Aberdeens holding a "Drawing Room" at St. Patrick's Hall in Dublin Castle gives some idea of the 'pomp and circumstances' of such affairs.[21]

Particularly when Lady Aberdeen was Vicereine, the wearing of Irish lace assumed a new importance socially. Lady Aberdeen held a Lace Ball in 1907 at which everyone was requested to wear Irish lace. Apart from obvious uses like

Left: Being presented at a 'Drawing Room' in Dublin Castle during the Vice-Royalty of the Marquis & Marchioness of Aberdeen. From Souvenir Album presented to them.

Right: Jane Vere O'Brien, daughter of Florence, wearing her dress and train for her presentation in 1909 at St. Patrick's Hall, Dublin Castle, during Lord Aberdeen's term as Viceroy. Photo: Rowe Collection.

Miss de Stacpoole's wedding, bridesmaids' and travelling gowns. Drawing from *Irish Society & Social Review*, 3rd Sept. 1902. Lent by Anita Puigcerver-Rumbold.

wedding veils and court trains the amount of lace worn on clothes for all social occasions was amazing. Anita Puigcerver-Rumbold, a descendent of the 9th Earl of Westmeath, has kindly lent me a scrap-book from this period which emphasises the sheer quantity of lace involved. The book belonged to Mrs May Nugent Popoff, Miss Puigcerver-Rumbold's great-aunt. The picture, taken from the scrapbook, of Miss de Stacpoole's wedding, bridesmaids' and travelling gowns, gives some idea of the amount of lace used: there were eight bridesmaids as well as two train-bearers.

Lace was also a treasured wedding gift. In April 1903 Miss Stapleton-Bretherton, on her marriage to Mr. Rowland Feilding, received gifts of lace from Lady Parker, Mr and Mrs Baxter, Mrs and Miss Lyon and Sister Mary of St. Thais.[22]

At the wedding of Arthur Edward Rogers of Oaklands, Clonmel, and Lily, third daughter of Sir John Arnott in Cork, the bride wore a charming dress of white crepe de chine, which was handsomely embroidered with real lace, manufactured in the Irish School of Art Needlework, Dublin. On the shoulders of the dress was a beautiful lace fichu, with an extremely pretty panel of lace embroidered from the neck of the gown to the flounce. The bridesmaids included Miss Bagwell (Marlfield) and Miss Frances Bagwell (Eastgrove), cousins of the bridegroom.[23]

Mrs Bagwell of Marlfield was the manager at this period of a coloured embroidery industry so would have had plenty of contacts with outlets like the School of Art Needlework.

Being presented to the Viceroy was as important in Irish society as being presented in Court to the King and Queen in London. The Court gowns were lace trimmmed and were worn with a long train which was often of lace or lace-trimmed.

Even at afternoon parties lace was worn. The August 1898 issue of *Irish Society* describes 'a most enjoyable and successful afternoon party at Dunsandle which was largely attended'. The guests included the Hon. E. Dillon who was 'charmingly dressed in white embroidered muslin trimmed with lace and finished with a wide yellow sash, her large white hat was ornamented with ostrich tips and bunches of yellow roses.' At the same function 'Mrs Wood's grey costume was finished with cream lace' and Mrs Persse of Roxboro 'looked very smart in a costume of white cloth, with toque composed of deep pink roses finished with black lace rosettes.'[24]

Lace Displays Today

The Irish Country Women's Association is the recipient of the proceeds of the Branchardiere Fund today. The fund was set up by Riego de la Branchardiere, a very successful lace designer, mostly of crochet, who had a studio in London. The first recipient in 1891 was the Women's National Health Association. Lady Aberdeen was very quick to look for any money that was being distributed. An Grianan, the headquarters of the Irish Countrywomen's Association, has some fine specimens of old lace. The Museum there is open only to residents of the College. Classes in lace making are held at An Grianan on a regular basis. In 1993 there was one course for Limerick lace, two for Carrickmacross, three for Youghal, as well as sessions for crochet and Mountmellick work. Applications for these residential courses should be made direct to An Grianan, Termonfeckin, Co. Louth.

Lace enthusiasts visiting Ireland should see the collections which are on display. Lace is still made at the Good Shepherd Convent in Limerick by a few elderly workers who use the traditional frames, but who make only darned-net, or run-work. Tambour lace-making does not appear to have survived after the early 1920s. The lace room at the Good Shepherd Convent is open for business in the tourist season. Most of us would love to receive any piece made there, even if it is not as elaborate as the beautiful christening robe given to the late President Kennedy.

At the National Museum in Kildare St., Dublin there are some fine specimens made in Cork and Limerick. Cork Public Museum at FitzGerald Park in the Mardyke, includes in its collection, a Limerick lace christening robe made in Cork about 1900. Kinsale Regional Museum has a sizable collection of lace and other needlework on permanent display; the Kinsale display includes photos of four pieces made at Kinsale which won First Prize at the Dublin Exhibition of 1897 and which were purchased by Queen Victoria. The work of individual lace-makers like Brigid Newman, Catherine Curran and Hannah Kelly from St. Joseph's Convent is recorded there. Other displays can be seen at the Limerick Museum, (see the child's apron pictured at page 13) the Crawford Municipal Art Gallery in Cork, The Ulster Folk and Transport Museum at Cultra, Hollywood, Co Down and at Monaghan Museum which specializes in the Carrickmacross lace made in the area. As the collections are not always on display it is as well to write in advance to give the date of one's visit. The Visitor Centre at Kenmare, Co. Kerry, has a very good display of Irish lace, including Limerick.

Notes

1. Undated hand-written account from Mrs Vere O'Brien's private papers.
2. *Ibid*.
3. Entire paragraph from Mrs Vere O'Brien's private papers.
4. Guide to the collection of lace – Ada K. Longfield (later Ada Leask). Published National Museum of Ireland 1970. Also from unsigned article dating from about 1850 given to Nellie Ó Cléirigh by Sister Marguerite of the Good Shepherd Convent in Limerick in December 1984.
5. *Ibid*.
6. Information supplied by Miss Dorothy Stewart, Limerick.
7. Information supplied by Sister Marguerite to Nellie Ó Cléirigh.
8. Catalogue of the Cork Exhibition 1883.
9. *A Renascence (sic) of the Irish Art of Lace-making*. A.S.C. (Alan S. Cole) reprint Ulster Folk & Transport Museum 1988.
10. *We Twa*. Reminiscences of Lord and Lady Aberdeen 1925.
11. *A Renascence* . . . as at 9 above.
12. Mrs Vere O'Brien's notes of conversations with older workers.
13. Information to Nellie Ó Cléirigh from Sister M. Imelda, Convent of Mercey, Kinsale in October 1983.
14. Mrs Vere O'Brien's private papers.
15. Information to Nellie Ó Cléirigh from Sister M. de Lourdes, Irish Sisters of Charity in September 1976.
16. Records of Congested Districts Board for Ireland (1891-1921) in Nellie Ó Cléirigh's possession.
17. Lectures by Professor Turpin of National College of Art, Dublin delivered to the Old Dublin Society and published in their Journal 1984-87.
18. Information from the Catalogue of the Chicago Fair of 1893, officially titled 'The World Columbian Exposition'.
19. Catalogue of Chicago Exhibition, 1893.
20. *Slainte*, the Journal of the Women's National Health Association of Ireland. Edited by the Countess of Aberdeen. Vol. 111, 1911.
21. Untitled newspaper cutting dated 11 July 1911. Lent by Anita Puigcerver-Rumbold to Nellie Ó Cléirigh.
22. Untitled newspaper cutting dated April 1903. Lent by Anita Puigcerver-Rumbold to Nellie Ó Cléirigh.
23. Untitled and undated newspaper cutting with papers from 1902 lent to Nellie Ó Cléirigh by Anita Puigcerver-Rumbold.
24. *Ibid*.

Part Two:
Florence Vere O'Brien and the
Limerick Lace School

'Old Church', Limerick, Robert & Florence's first home. Rowe Collection.

Top: Florence Vere O'Brien, 1883. Rowe Collection.

Below: Robert Vere O'Brien, 1883. Rowe Collection.

Florence was twenty-nine when, in 1883, she arrived in Limerick with her newly wed husband, Robert Vere O'Brien, younger son of the Hon. Robert O'Brien and nephew of the thirteenth Lord Inchiquin, of Dromoland.[1] It was not her first time to visit the city, as she and Robert had first met at a charity ball in Limerick in 1878 when Florence had been on a tour of Ireland, and had stayed as a guest at Tervoe House, home of Lord and Lady Emly. Married life started for the young couple at 'Oldchurch', a large house on the Clare side of the River Shannon, near Barrington's Pier, Limerick, which they shared with Robert's mother, Mrs. Ellen Vere O'Brien and his sister Alice.

Florence's background was an interesting one. Her father, William Arnold, was a son of Dr Thomas Arnold of Rugby, and a brother of Matthew Arnold the poet. William had been Director of Education of the Punjab in India, where, in 1858, his wife Frances died leaving him with four small chlldren. They were sent home the following year on the *SS Calcutta* to Yorkshire to live with William's sister Jane and her husband, William E. Forster. A few weeks later William Arnold left India to join his children, became ill aboard ship, died and was buried at Gibraltar, at the age of thirty-one. So in a matter of a few months, Florence, her two brothers and her sister were left orphans, the eldest, her brother Edward, being only seven years old.[2]

The children were, however, extremely fortunate in their adoptive parents, Jane and William E. Forster. It would be hard to imagine a more loving and kindly home, or one in which hard work and service to the community were taken more for granted. Indeed, when they reached their twenties, so high was their regard for Jane and William, that they took on the name Forster, and henceforward were known as Arnold-Forster.

William E. Forster, the only son of Quaker parents, with his partner William Fison, ran a woollen mill at Burley-in-Wharfedale, in Yorkshire, as a family concern, involving the workers as friends. Entering politics, Forster became Minister for Education in Gladstone's Liberal government, and in 1880 was sent to Ireland as Chief Secretary. Here he and his family spent two years in the Chief Secretary's lodge (now the residence of the American Ambassador) in Phoenix Park.[3] During this time Florence met and helped to entertain a wide and varied political and social circle of visitors; but managed none-the-less to keep up her contact with Robert Vere O'Brien.[4] Early in 1883 Robert proposed to Florence in London, and they were married later in the same year.

Through her family and connections Florence came to Limerick armed with a wide knowledge of people, politics, literature and education, and above all, a strong sense of duty to help in any community in which she might find herself. She was also very artistic and had studied drawing in London with several well-known teachers. Her first encounter with the Limerick lace-makers was at Limerick railway station. She writes that the Limerick lace, 'chiefly sold as such at the railway station, and in the streets as well as in the shops, though often good in workmanship, and sometimes in design, was apt to be made in such coarse materials as to be more suitable for furniture than for flounces or for handkerchiefs.'

Through this initial contact Florence became interested in the history of lace making in Limerick. Since the introduction of lace making by Mr Walker and his band of teachers from Coggeshall in 1829 the industry had had its ups and downs.[5] Limerick lace had been extremely popular with Queen Victoria and her ladies during the 1840s and '50s. In writing to Pierre Verhaegen of Ghent (a provincial councillor and author of a large work on Belgian lace-making) in 1901, describing the Limerick Lace industry, Florence says: 'Indeed to hear the fond reminiscences of some of my old workers, one would imagine that in the halcyon days of the forties Queen Victoria and all the ladies of the Court went about in garments draped principally in Limerick lace literally from head to foot, for I have in my possession, among my specimans, not only vests and capes, but infants' socks made in lace and bearing a design of shamrock and harp.' However the trade suffered a decline when the death of Prince Albert in 1861 plunged the court into mourning. Whether this was the reason or not it was certainly from about this date that the decline in fashion for lace began. Also the introduction of machine made lace from Nottingham affected the industry. Yet in spite of these set-backs Limerick lace never became extinct. Fortunately Mr Walker and his successors had provided the workers with an excellent training, both in design and craftmanship. The best designs, and the best net and threads available, had been imported from Brussels. In 1877 Cannocks of George's Street were still employing seventy women. Along with Todds of William Street, and the Convent of the Good Shepherd, these workrooms continued to produce tambour and run lace, a great part of which was for ecclesiastical and theatrical use, though some lace for dress purposes was also made. These centres were still in business in 1883 when Florence arrived in Limerick, but the demand for the finer kind of lace was so small that the principal employers did not consider it worth their while to go to the expense of importing high quality materials.

Florence quickly realised that there was a need for better materials and good designs, and help was forthcoming from her husband's aunt, Lady de Vere of Curragh Chase,[6] near Adare, Co. Limerick, who supplied some fine old Brussels net and thread. These were inherited from the former Lady de Vere, Robert's maternal grandmother, who in the 1840s had run a school for so-called 'Curragh lace'. Here a type of appliqué lace, from Point d'Alencon designs, was made.[7] A neighbour of Florence in Limerick, Madame O'Grady, lent an old lace design, and Mary Blake, one of the old Limerick lace-workers, was persuaded to work a 'run lace' flounce on the Brussels net. This first piece was paid for by Robert, and presented to Florence. Gradually some of the old workers, who had been trained when children, in Forrest's factory, including Peggy Kiely, whose memory reached back to Mr Walker's day, came to Florence for materials and designs. They would take these home and 'employ all the technical skill and intelligence which made them so delightful to deal with as workwomen'.

Florence's involvement in the improvement of lace must be seen against the background of the revival of interest in craftmanship and design which was taking place in England and elsewhere during the late 19th Century. Inspired in England by Augustus Pugin, John Ruskin, Henry Cole, and most importantly, by William Morris, a number of groups and guilds concerned with the crafts were founded during this period. These included the Art Workers Guild, the Arts and Crafts Exhibition Society, the Home Arts and Industries Association, and the Queen's Institute for the Training and Employment of Educated Women. As Ireland was politically and culturally attached to England, some of these organisations soon had their counterparts in Ireland.[8] By the end of the 1800s Lord Mayo had started the Irish Arts and Crafts Society, and Horace Plunkett had initiated the co-operative movement. Unemployment was such that efforts were made in a number of different places throughout the country to establish cottage industries. In Limerick, Florence, in many ways, seems to have been the right person in the right place at the right time.

During the same year, 1883, in which Florence arrived in Limerick, other events of significance to the lace industry were taking place there. An art exhibition, held in the Athenaeum meeting rooms, was the occasion for several lectures on the need for improvement in art and design, given by Mr Alan Cole, an expert in needle-

Limerick tambour lace flounce – an award winning design by Emily Anderson in the 1886 competition: made by Mrs Vere O'Brien's workers. From *A Renascence of the Irish Art of Lace Making* by Alan Cole, 1888.

work from the Department of Science and Art , South Kensington, London. Alan Cole's father, Sir Henry Cole was the founding father of the South Kensington Museum which later became the Victoria and Albert Museum. From Limerick Alan Cole travelled to Cork where a major Exhibition of Irish Manufactures was in progress, and where he gave some more lectures. He pointed out the far higher standard of design of some old pieces of lace on loan from the South Kensington Museum, compared to those on view at the Exhibition. Following these lectures the Cork Exhibition Committee urged the Department of Science and Art to continue giving lectures, and lending specimens of old lace to lace-making schools at convents and elsewhere. In a year or two several convents had established art classes, and Alan Cole was commissioned to visit and inspect their work. Subsequently the 'Private Committee for Promoting Irish Lace' was formed in 1884 to raise money to offer prizes for lace designs. Among the earliest subscribers to this committee were Edward William O'Brien of Cahirmoyle, Co Limerick, a cousin of Robert Vere O'Brien, Lord Emly, in whose house Robert and Florence had met, and Lord Monteagle of Mount Trenchard,[9] another family connection of the O'Briens through the de Vere family. Obviously Florence was going to get all the encouragement and help possible from these people in her efforts to improve the lace industry.

The work of the Private Committee to improve designs through competitions proved very successful. Sixty-seven designers entered the competitions in 1886, submitting 200 designs, of which fifty were awarded prizes.[10]

As her experiments progressed Florence looked further afield for materials and designs. She imported fine net from Brussels, and thread from Marshall of Leeds, and later from Nottingham and Chesterfield. Some of her designs came from rubbings she made of old lace lent to her by friends, and redrawn for the workers' use, and some were original. Later there was the valuable addition of designs from the Schools of Art in London, Cork and Limerick. Miss Emily Anderson of the School of Art in Cork, Mr Michael Hayes of Limerick, and Miss Farman of Leicester, produced some of the most successful designs, and were prizewinners in the competitions organised in 1885 and 1886 by the Private Committee for the Promotion of Irish Lace. Mr Brenan, Head of the School of Art in Cork, was a continual support and help in the matter of design. He and Florence met for the first time in Cork in 1886, after several years of correspondence. Encouragement

came not only from Alan Cole and Mr Brenan, but also from Mrs Power-Lalor (who had been appointed Lace Inspector for Ireland), and from Mr Biddle, of Haywards in Oxford Street, London, whose advice and orders were very valuable. Mr Ben Lindsey's Irish Lace Depot, Dublin, and later Lady Aberdeen's Irish Industries Association depots, both in London and Dublin, were important sales outlets.

Alan Cole visited Limerick in 1886, and was taken by Florence to visit some of the old workers. Using some of the new prizewinning lace designs, commissions had been worked for Queen Victoria (the Queen's flounce being made from a design by Miss Farman of Leicester), the Countess of Aberdeen, and Mrs Alfred Morrison, all enthusiastic supporters of the use of fine lace. By now Florence had persuaded the Convent of the Good Shepherd to become more seriously involved in the making of lace, and was providing them with better designs. Florence's description of her own group of lace workers from this time is worth quoting:

Limerick run-lace scarf designed by Mrs. Vere O'Brien and made by her lace makers. From *A Renascence of the Irish Art of Lace Making* by Alan Cole, 1887.

'These workers enter with the greatest intelligence into the idea of a new design, which we used to examine together before it was worked, either at my own house, or in their own little rooms – rooms often so dark and dingy in the most dilapidated quarter of the so-called 'English town' of Limerick, that it was a wonder how the lace could emerge, as it generally did, as clean and fresh as if made in the most well-appointed and roomy factory. Sometimes I am bound to say, there were difficulties peculiar to cottage industries. Turf smoke in excess, a drunken husband, and once a cat who jumped through a beautlful 'run lace' flounce, when in the frame, to the bitter disappointment of both the worker and myself.'

Following this visit Alan Cole reported that Florence's lace makers were kept very busy, and also that sales of the less expensive kinds produced and sold by Messrs Cannocks – leading drapers and milliners – had considerably increased, and that altogether about 110 lacemakers were now employed in Limerick.[11]

The year 1887 was a busy time for Florence: as well as her lace business she and Robert now had two sons, Aubrey and Hugh, and many social engagements. Robert was Clerk of the Peace at Ennis Courthouse, which, with his other commitments as, for example, agent of the Inchiquin and the De Vere Estates, kept him continually traveling on the roads of Clare and Limerick. Often he would come home exhausted after a long, cold, wet drive, and would have to set off again the following morning.[12] When the assizes were held in Kilrush, Florence and Robert loved to take the opportunity of a few days in Kilkee, sometimes on their own and sometimes with the family, renting a lodge overlooking the sea, or staying in Moore's Hotel. Here he and Florence would read aloud to each other, and take long walks along the cliffs. Robert was the ideal partner for her enterprises, always encouraging and practical, and helping to deal calmly with problems as they arose. She always said that without Robert's strong support behind her she never could have achieved all she did with the Limerick lace. She describes him as the 'foundation and corner stone' of all her activities.

In 1888 Florence went with Robert on a short visit to three convents in Cork where Limerick Lace was now made. For the past few years she had been in correspondence with these convents in connection with designs and materials. She now had the opportunity for the first time of meeting the sisters of Mercy at the Convent of St Vincent, the Convent of the Good Shepherd at Sunday's Well, and St Joseph's Convent at Kinsale, where she was impressed with the quality of work being done. Kinsale she describes as a 'very picturesque, but poverty stricken town', and remarked that 'I do not know how Ireland would get on without the Convents and the Convent Industrial Schools'.

In October of 1888 an important event took place: Alan Cole was once again in Limerick to give a lecture, and show a small collection of lace. Lord Emly was in the Chair, and Donough O'Brien[13], a first cousin of Robert, helped to organise the meeting. Alan Cole spoke of the work of the committees that had been set up, and the art classes started in Cork, since his 1883 lecture there. He suggested that Florence Vere O'Brien should have help in the work that she was doing in improving the lace making industry in Limerick. Through her efforts, he said 'leading dealers in London readily take from her quantities of her lace'; and now was the time for a working committee to be formed. Its first step should be to set up a drawing class for young lace workers. Alan Cole suggested that the Limerick School of Art should now consider starting classes in lace design. Prizes for lace design offered by the Royal Dublin Society for the first time that year, had as their principal objective, the encouragement of the production of new patterns by local designers. At the end of the meeting Mr Alexander Shaw, a leading Limerick businessman, offered £50 towards the starting of a lace teaching society, and Florence was asked if she would call a committee to see what should be the next step.[14]

A committee was duly formed consisting of Robert and Florence Vere O'Brien, Mr. Donough O'Brien, Mr Shaw, Mr Murray of Todds, Mr Moran of Cannocks and Mr Brophy of the School of Art, and met at Mr Donough O'Brien's office. An appeal was launched inviting people to become members of a general council; and in December the society was formally launched with £100, and with support from Bishop O'Dwyer, Lord Emly, Mr O'Donnell, the High Sherriff, Lady Limerick, and Mr Bannatyne.

The lace training school, managed by the committee, opened with eight pupils in May 1889 in two small rooms at the top of a house in Bank Place. Miss Caman was the Superintendent and tambour teacher, Mrs Keane (one of Florence's workers) being the run-lace teacher. By June there were twenty pupils on the books; and Alan Cole called to see the school on his tour of inspection in October.

Florence and Robert's first daughter Jane[15] was born in November, 1889, and six months later, in May 1890, the O'Brien family moved from Oldchurch to New Hall, a large house just south-west of Ennis, in County Clare, which they rented from the McDonnell family. This was mainly to enable Robert to be close to his work at Ennis Courthouse. However, it also meant that Florence now had to travel about twenty-five miles to Limerick, either by train or horse drawn vehicle, to continue her involvement with the new committee, and with her lace workers.

It must be said at this stage that Florence was never short of help in running her household. In the move to New Hall she was accompanied by her sister-in-law and 'three of the maids'. Her staff would have included a nursery maid, housemaids and a cook as well as a gardener. Later there would be a governess. The achievements of an active and talented person such as Florence depended on the smooth working of a loyal group of people in the background.

During a visit to Limerick by Lady Aberdeen in 1892, when she was making arrangements for the 'Irish Village' to be held at the 1893 Chicago World Columbian Exposition, she visited the Lace Training School, and reported that 'It

consisted of two rooms in an old building in a squalid part of the city. There were perhaps twenty girls being taught there to make Limerick Lace, which threatened to become a lost art until a number of ladies and gentlemen conceived the idea of having the children taught by the surviving lace makers'. The school appears to have been flourishing, and Lady Aberdeen presented prizes to some of the girls, and one lace maker was selected for the 'Irish Village'. She was also shown the lace being prepared for the Chicago Exhibition.[16] An account of these exhibits appears in the *Limerick Chronicle* of 24 June 1893: 'We are glad to notice that Limerick will uphold its name at the World Fair for its lace – lace not made elsewhere but by local operatives. The Lace School, which since its formation some years ago, has been doing such an important work in reviving the Limerick Lace industry, will be well represented at the Exhibition, and in addition to this, another consignment is being sent out by Mrs R. Vere O'Brien, who, it is unnecessary to say, has taken for a long time past the livliest interest in the matter of lace-work. Mrs O'Brien has had constantly employed a number of workers who represent some of the old factory hands of bye-gone days, and has just turned out several exquisite specimens. These have been on view during the last few days at the house of Mrs Rice, New Street, under whose supervision the work has been carried on. One and all of the several specimens, are each beautiful works of art – the floral ornamentation is delicately traced, and some old designs have been reproduced in a most perfect and skillful manner. A number of ladies have seen the lace during the past few days, and bestowed on it the highest praise. There are four beautiful specimens of tambour work to match. One is a curtain for a baby's cot, and another a quilt lined with satin and wadded. We also noticed in tambour work a very pretty flounce of a trellis pattern, worked on a very clear net. Another exhibit is a reproduction in tambour of old Brussels lace, and we also observed a rich and heavy pattern in cream colour worked on Bretonne net. In black lace is a beautiful specimen to which trailing flowers are worked out in a most artistic manner, and a narrow black flounce in tambour work may also be mentioned. A scarf of very striking design in white lace is also on view. It shows a dragon at each corner, with a harp in the centre, whilst shamrocks are plentifully interspersed throughout. A very handsome white Bretonne scarf of floral pattern with bunches of drooping berries, deserves special mention, as also a fichu copied from Chantilly lace. Amongst the other articles are a handkerchief in needlerun lace, which is a very pretty idea; a cream coloured fan

Medal awarded to "Mrs. Vere O'Brien's industry" at the World Columbian Exposition, Chicago 1892-93. Rowe Collection. Photo: Judith Badman.

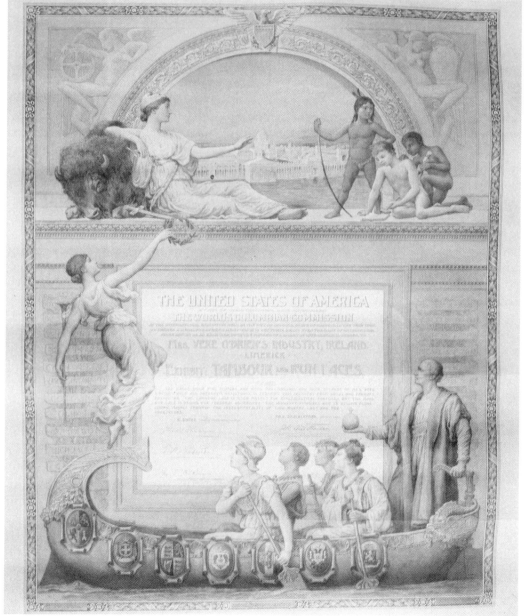

Certificate awarded to the Limerick Lace-making School, for its entry of Creme Blonde Lace Scarf, at the World Columbian International Exhibition (*sic*) Chicago, 1893. Rowe Collection. Photo: David Rowe.

cover – needlerun – copied from Chantilly lace; and two Limerick blonde scarfs, worked in cream floss – silk, which deservedly came in for special attention. One of these is a copy of old Spanish lace, and the other a new drawing. Over one hundred pounds worth, the work of old hands, as they are termed, to distinguish them from the lace school, will be sent out to Chicago, and, judging by the varied character of the exhibits, and their undoubtedly high merit, we have no doubt they will meet with a ready sale, and that further consignments will be required later on from Limerick.' Both the 'Lace making School' and 'Mrs Vere O'Brien's Industry' were awarded medals at the Fair.

The Lace Training School continued for three years, but running it by a committee was not a very satisfactory arrangement, and in March 1893 Florence was formally asked by Mr Shaw if she would consider taking over complete responsibility for the school. She agreed to this and the Training School was formally closed and handed over to Florence, who opened her own 'Limerick Lace School' on 6 November 1893, at 112 George's Street (now O'Connell. Street), with Miss Dunne as Manageress, Mrs Rice as Superintendent and Mary Kenna and Cathy Bowles as teachers. This new school opened with 'five little girls as pupils'. Judging from the photographs the children must have started at about thirteen or fourteen years of age.

She writes in her diary: 'This school is entirely Robert's and my private venture, unconnected with the committee school at Bank Place, to which it succeeds by amicable arrangement. It costs Robert about 30s. a week, a very heavy expense and one which I cannot expect him to continue.' (This would have been equivalent to about £85 in 1993.) 'Meantime the school – and depot which it gives me – are a great interest to me, and I am fortunate in having two such excellent co-adjutors as Mrs. Rice and Miss Dunne. In the last year we sold altogether £500 [about £28,500 in 1993] worth of lace – but £100 of this was from the Chicago exhibition (through Lady Aberdeen's Irish Industries Association) and will not occur again. Meantime we keep our thirty old workers (externs) in constant employment, and if it were not for the school we should pay our way.' Of the new school, Florence explains in a letter to the *Limerick Chronicle* of June 1894: 'The object of the school, as at present carried on, is to give free instruction in lace making to young girls who may wish to take up the industry in after life, either at

Left: Miss Norah Dunne, manageress of the Limerick Lace School. Rowe Collection.

Right: Mrs. Rice, superintendent of the Limerick Lace School. Rowe Collection.

their own homes or in one or other of the existing factories in the city.' She adds: 'We also have a "paying class" in connection with the school for any person who may wish to avail themselves of the services of our experienced teachers, and to make use of the frames provided at the school.'

In the meantime Florence's lace business was steadily growing. Her account books, meticulously kept by Robert, record sales increasing from £30. 7s. 7d. in 1885 to £889. 0s. 11d. in 1898 [equivalent to about £50,000 in 1993 money]. In that year a profit was recorded for the first time, and amounted to £70. 6s. 5d. [about £4000 in 1993 money].

Of wage levels Florence wrote in 1897: 'My own outside workers number now only about thirty, and we have eight young girls learning in the school, who have been taught gratis, and the best of whom can now earn 7s. per week [about £20 in 1993 money]. A small sum enough if regarded as the wages of a breadwinner, but not contemptible as the earnings of a young girl with no corresponding expenditure, and working only six hours a day. Obviously we are on a very small scale, and moreover Limerick Lace as an Irish industry has many rivals to contend with and many difficulties to encounter from the counter-attractions of America, the preference of many girls for the greatersociability and independence of factory life, and the low rate of wages (1s. 6d. a day, about £4 in 1993 money) made necessary by the competition of women workers in Switzerland and Belgium, whose cheap labour would quickly induce our best employers to abandon the small Limerick Lace School, if they were expected to give orders as a charity to the highest bidder.' The number of workers employed in lacemaking in Belgium in 1896 was stated as 47,571![17]

Retail prices varied greatly, according to the quality, size and complexity of the work; but some idea may be gained from the following (which is extracted from 1906 account books): handkerchiefs ranging from 4s.6d. to 9s. each [1993: about £13 to £26]; flounces from 10s. 2d. per yard to 14s. 8d. [1993: about £29 to £41]; trimming lace, 3s. 8d. per yard [1993: about £10]; fan covers from 11s. 4d. to 17s. [1993: about £33 to £48]; a three-yard run lace scarf, £3.3s. [1993: about £190]; and a bridal veil, £7.15s. [1993: about £445]. But the profit margins must have been very small: for example, a fan cover selling at 17s. [1993: £48] involved 12s. [1993: £34] for labour and 3s. [1993: £8] for materials, leaving only 2s. [1993: £6] for overheads.

Sales were promoted by exhibitions, which were numerous in the 1890s, both in Ireland and in England. £100 worth of goods [1993: about £5700] were sold at Lady Aberdeen's Irish Industries Association stall at the Chicago Exhibition, in 1893. These exhibitions were the chief means of selling the high quality hand made lace, and were mainly organised by the Irish Industries Association. Sales were held in private houses and halls, and the stalls were looked after by ladies who gave their time and energy voluntarily. Fashion in the 1890s favoured lace, and sales were high.

The Dublin Science and Art Department bought two pieces of lace from the Limerick Lace School, in 1898, for the museum in Kildare Street. One of these was Florence's own design and worked by Mary Kenna. At the Dublin Horse Show in August 1898 the Limerick Lace School took first prize for a lace skirt, which was then bought by Lady Cadogan.

In the following month, September 1898, the family, now with four children, their second daughter Florence (known as Flora) having been born in 1896, moved again, this time from New Hall to Ballyalla, a house which they bought three miles north of Ennis, which was to be the O'Brien family home until the 1950s.

Florence undertook to organise the combined lace stall at Lady Arran's Windsor Sale in 1900. This involved a great deal of writing to various convents, and other lace centres, about their contributions. Finally she and Miss Dunne travelled to Windsor with hundreds of pounds worth of lace for the stall. Queen Victoria attended this sale in her wheelchair, and bought a scarf, described by Florence as 'my best piece of black lace, made by Maggie O'Driscoll.' The Princess of Wales

A Limerick tambour lace flounce acquired by the National Museum, Dublin in 1888. Catalogue to the collection of lace: Ada Longfield.

came next day and bought a white scarf, made by Brigid Doody. This sort of royal patronage greatly helped to sell the lace; and £200 worth [1993: about £12,000] was sold in two afternoons at Windsor.

About this time the Lace School moved its premises from 112 to 48 George's. Street, where it remained until its final closure in 1922.

In 1901 negotiations were in progress for the starting of art classes for the lace workers. The proposal which had first come from Mr Alan Cole at his lecture in 1888, was only now being taken up by the new Department of Agriculture and Technical Instruction with the encouragement of Miss Emily Anderson, now an instructor, and Mr Rich, the Department Inspector. Mr Clark, who assisted Mr Brophy, the Head of the Limerick School of Art, was in favour of the proposal, and Miss Dunne, Manageress of the Limerick Lace school, said that twenty of the pupils would be ready to join the class. Mr Murray of Todds and Mr Kidmarsh of Cannocks, who handled through their stores the less expensive end of the lace market, agreed to allow some of their lace making employees to attend the classes. These classes were therefore inaugurated, and subsequently some of the designs produced were used by Florence in her lace business.

An exhibit from Florence's Limerick Lace School won first prize in 1902 at the Royal Dublin Society Industries Exhibition, but she says that Limerick Lace 'has now many rivals and no longer holds the field as it did at one time.' Many of the

"Ballyalla", home of O'Brien family from 1898. Rowe Collection.

Fan cover designed by Florence Vere O'Brian c. 1900. Roew Collection. Photo: Judith Badman.

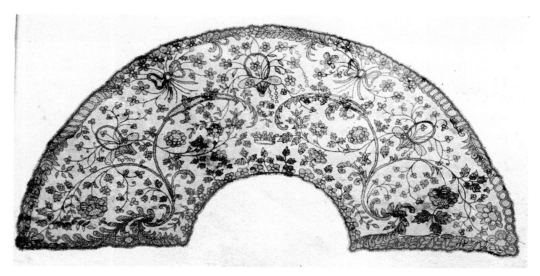

Fan designed by Florence Vere O'Brien for Lady Cadogan, 1901. Rowe Collection.

convents and lace centres round the country made 'Limerick' as well as other varieties of lace. Limerick lace was represented at the Co. Clare stand, at a sale in aid of the City of Dublin Hospital, 1902. There were thirteen lace centres entered for the Royal Dublin Society 'Limerick Lace, Tambour and Run Section' in 1903, but, despite the competition, Florence's Limerick Lace School again won first prize,

The Lace School, Limerick. *The Ladies Field*, 1899. Rowe Collection.

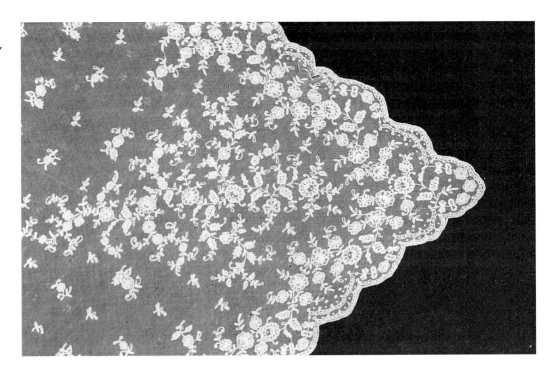

Detail of Limerick tambour lace bridal veil, c. 1900. Rowe Collection. Photo: Norman Campion.

this time for a bridal veil.[18]

Classes in Limerick Lace making were now being given at twenty convents and other centres round the country, the leading centres being Florence Vere O'Brien's Limerick Lace School and the Mercy Convent in Kinsale.

One of Florence's most successful 'bread and butter' lines was the Limerick Lace motor veil, which was advertised in the *Motoring Illustrated* of June 1903, as 'guaranteed to wash like a handkerchief' and cost from 15s. [1993: about £43]. The Clare Journal was enthusiastic, and said that 'good lace may be dust-begrimed, mudspattered or wet through, but the laundress or cleaner readily restores it to its pristine freshness and beauty'!

Limerick run lace handkerchief, sample book. Rowe Collection.

Limerick lace at the Clare stand in aid of the City of Dublin Hospital, Dublin 1902. Rowe Collection.

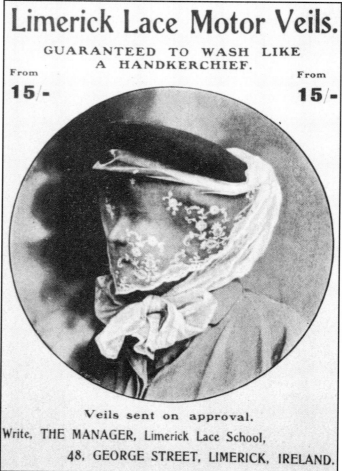

Advertisement from the *Motoring Illustrated*, 1903. Rowe Collection.

During the same year lace workers and others were busy preparing for the great exhibition to be held at St. Louis, U.S.A. in April 1904. The Limerick papers described a bridal costume of Limerick Tambour being sent by the Limerick Lace School, made of ecru lace mounted on white chiffon with a foundation of white silk. The design of the lace included daisies, maidenhair ferns, shamrock, thistles and roses, and the sleeves and sides were held by gold buttons and links. The skirt was made of a deep flounce of lace and the coat was of a long open pattern.[19] This exhibit was awarded a silver medal at St. Louis, and another medal was awarded for a tea gown designed by Josephine Murphy, and made by Mary Kenna of the Limerick Lace School.[20]

The return of the Liberal Government in England in 1906 brought the Aberdeens back from Canada to the Vice-Regal Lodge in Dublin, and Lady Aberdeen was immediately in the thick of all matters relating to the arts and crafts. She was at the Limerick Lace School in February, where she bought a veil to wear on the train of her first Drawing Room dress of the season, and promptly ordered a second one to match. The Daily Chronicle recorded the event: 'Her Excellency's dress for the first Drawing Room to-night is not only made in the Irish capital, but is completely covered with a mass of Irish hand embroidery, worked in silver

Above: Silver medal, Louisiana Purchase Exposition, 1904. Rowe Collection. Photo: Judith Badman.

Right: Certificate of the Universal Exposition, St. Louis, 1904, commemorating the acquisition of the Louisiana territory. In respect of a silver medal for tea gown of Limerick lace. Rowe Collection.

Right: Limerick tambour lace tea gown, c. 1900. Rowe Collection. Photo: Peter Lamb.

Detail of tambour lace tea gown. Rowe Collection. Photo: Peter Lamb.

bugles and applied to grey satin. The grey velvet train will be draped with a square of very fine Limerick lace made for the occasion at Mrs Vere O'Brien's lace school in Limerick.'[21] It is not surprising that with all these successes, the Corporation of Limerick authorised the use of the city arms as a badge of excellence to Florence's Limerick Lace School.[22]

In addition to the lace workers employed in convents and for the Limerick shops, Florence was now keeping fifty-six workers in constant employment, and a good worker could earn up to 14s. a week [1993: about £40]. 'The Limerick Lace School' was used as the address from which all Florence's lace was sold, whether it was made by the older workers in their own homes, or by the young workers on the premises.

Florence Vere O'Brien with her daughters Flora (left) and Jane, the author's mother, 1905. Rowe Collection.

Limerick Lace School,
1907. Rowe Collection.

By 1907 the industry had grown to such an extent that there were over eighty centres all over Ireland involved in making lace and crochet.[23] Despite the competition the School continued to win awards: at the International Exhibition in Dublin in 1907 it won a first prize.

Writing about the Ideal Homes Exhibition in London in 1908 an English newspaper draws attention 'to the very fine lace work shown, particularly from Ireland. The display from Mrs Vere O'Brien's Lace School at Limerick is a surprising proof of what cottagers can do when properly trained. Many of the specimens shown by her have a daintiness and exquisite finish worthy of the highest praise'.[24] In June 1908 at the Franco-British Exhibition at Sheperd's Bush in London, the Limerick Lace School was awarded a gold medal; at the Home Arts Exhibition, a gold cross. As Florence says 'Our merits have been fully recognised'! Sadly these golden awards seem to have disappeared.

On July 3rd 1908 Florence and Robert celebrated their twenty-fifth wedding anniversary. The presents that must have given Florence very special pleasure were two small pieces of lace, one run and the other tambour, made for her by the Limerick Lace School girls and by the older workers. These were accompanied by two letters with all their signatures.

Two years later Mrs Rice, the School Superintendent, died. She and Miss Dunne had worked together as a splendid team, and it was to these people and to Miss Dunne's nieces, Eileen and Brigid O'Donohue, who eventually took over the management, that so much of the success of the Limerick Lace School was due. Florence seems to have had a way of working with people that inspired continued affection and loyalty. Eileen O'Donohue, when considering taking another job in

Mrs. Vere O'Briens Lace School
48 George St
Limerick.

1.90

To Mrs Vere O'Brien
Dear Madam
Having heard that July 10th is the 25th anniversary of your marriage day, the pupils, Miss Fitzgerald, my sister, and I wish to offer our very best congratulations to you and Mr. Vere O'Brien and hope both of you will have many happy returns of the day.
We beg to take this opportunity of thanking you very sincerely for all you have done of Irish Industry particularly for Limerick Lace and for all you have done for us in admitting us into your Limerick Lace Training

School where we have been taught to make the best lace and through your exertions in finding a market for the work we can have permanent employment and earn good wages.
Owing to your great talent for design and needle-work the lace has been brought to the highest state of perfection so, when put before the public it never fails to be appreciated.
Wishing you, Mr Vere O'Brien and all the family every future happiness and prosperity, and hoping God will spare you to carry out the same good work you have so ably carried on for so many years we, the undersigned, beg you will accept the enclosed small piece of Limerick Run Lace made by one

of the workers trained in your school:

Margaret O'Driscoll   Bridget Clohessy
Ellie White   Bridget Kennedy
Teresa Lysaight   Mary E. Whelan
Agnes Campbell   Nellie Halpin
Nellie Delger   Josie Cooney
Mary Downey   Mary McCormack
Eileen Downey   Rosie Mahony
Alicia Wood   May McMahon
Mary Matthews   Mary J. Leo
Margaret Matthews   Eileen M. O'Donohue
Katie Moloney   Angela Kennedy
Madge O'Neill

Mary Fitzgerald - teacher.
Bridget Dunne - teacher
Norah Dunne - Manageress.

July 10th 1908.

To. Mrs. Vere O'Brien.   Limerick. 1908.

Dear Madam,

Having heard that the 15th July is the Twenty Fifth Anniversary of your Wedding Day. We the undersigned "Old Tambour Workers". Respectfully request your acceptance of this piece of Tambour Lace. And we also desire to offer you our Grateful Thanks for all your kindly interest in our welfare.

Since you came amongst us, you have kept a large number of Workers in constant employment, at a fare rate of wages. and in times of need, you have generously assisted us. We hope you and Mr. O'Brien, and all your Family, may be spared many years together in Health and Happiness.

Mary Monahan   Kate Connell
Anne Considine   Mary McNamara
Mary Donoghue   Alice Cooper
Bgt Donoghue.   Kate Skehan
Ellen Donoghue   Kate Oneill
Kate Bowles   Jane Butler
Kate Vaughan.   Mgt O'Brien .

E. Rice.

1919, wrote to Florence for advice as 'my friend, as well as my employer'. (Shades of W.E.Forster and the Burley Mill workers!) One of Florence's greatest gifts was her ability to be at ease with all sorts of people, and in the days when social differences were very clearly defined this was a great asset. She was as much at home with visiting dignitaries, or the county gentry, as she was with her youngest lace worker. She had many friends amongst the convents, and equally amongst the clergy of all persuasions. Politically she had been brought up as a Liberal Unionist, but sympathised with the many Nationalist members of her husband's family. Showing her work at a fund raising event for the Feis Ceoil in Ennis she remarks on how fortunate it is that embroidery 'is a non-contentious subject'! As her experience grew she was more and more in demand as a judge of lace and needlework, and was called upon to help at various exhibitions around the country.

In May 1913 Robert died, aged seventy-one, after a number of years of ill health. His last visit with Florence was to Monare, their holiday house on Foynes Island, in the Shannon estuary, given to Robert by his uncle, Sir Stephen de Vere, in 1890, and where they had spent many happy holidays. Robert had been Clerk of the Peace for County Clare for forty-nine years, only resigning in 1911. Theirs had been an ideal partnership in all ways. After Robert's death Florence continued with her designing, correspondence and visits to the Lace School, and by now many other activities, including her 'Clare Embroidery' class run from her home at Ballyalla.

War clouds were gathering, and war was declared in August 1914. 'During the war' Florence writes, 'the school practically ceased to exist, all the workers being dispersed to other employment, and the demand for lace having ceased'. This comment seems to overstate the position a little. In 1916 the income of the Lace School was £225. 9s. 4d. [1993: about £9000] and expenses were £266. 6s. 4d. [1993:

Design for Limerick Lace stole by E. O'Donohue, 1914. The enlarged detail below shows her initials in the bottom right hand corner. Confusingly, she signed herself variously Eily, Eileen and Aileen. Rowe Collection Photo: Judith Badman.

Limerick run lace stole made from E. O'Donohue design. Rowe Collection. Photo: Colin Smythe.

about £10,600]. In 1917 a small profit of £31. 8s. [1993: about £1250] appears to have been made.[25] However, times were hard, and Miss Nora Dunne, the faithful manageress since 1893, volunteered: 'I will reduce my wages [from 28s.] to 20s. per week [1993: from £56 down to about £40] (till times get better).' She died in 1918, but her nieces, Eileen and Brigid O'Donohue, took over the running of the now tiny depot and school. Eileen was a competent designer, and had contributed designs to the school between 1910 and 1914. Their letters to Florence between 1918 and 1920 described the difficulties of keeping going with small orders and rising costs, although in 1918 Eileen wrote, optimistically: 'I feel sure that this year will be the best we have had for some time.' However, during part of that year she took a teaching appointment with the Department of Agriculture and Technical Instruction, and gave classes at the Cork School of Art, and in Bantry and Youghal. In July 1919 Eileen left Limerick to take up an an assistant managership in a large hosiery company in Cork. Her sister Brigid continued in charge of the Lace School, which did not finally close its doors until 1922, when all the stocks, designs and materials were returned to Florence's home, Ballyalla. Two lace workers, Mary Fitzgerald (tambour) and Agnes Campbell (run lace), continued for a year or two to execute orders, and it is recorded that the first prize for lace at the Dublin Horse Show in 1923 went to the Limerick Lace School for a scarf aptly named 'Curragh' – the name of the De Vere house near Adare, from which Florence acquired her first designs and materials.

*

With the closure of the Lace School, Florence concentrated her efforts on her other interests. She restarted her 'Clare Embroidery' class at Ballyalla, with the continued help of Mina Keppie, a Scotswoman, who had originally joined the family as a children's nurse in 1887. Florence became involved in providing help for ex-servicemen in County Clare, and in fund raising for Lady Aberdeen's Women's National Health Association. She continued her interests in the local sanatorium and the district nurse scheme.[26] To the end, despite failing health, Florence maintained her interest in people and politics, and her enjoyment of elegant clothes. (She was remembered, even in her later years, as being always beautifully dressed). She loved her family, her Clare home, her garden and her books. On her death in July 1936 *The Times*, describing her as 'the last of the granddaughters of Dr Arnold of Rugby', wrote: 'Her gentle, unselfish service, rooted in a deep piety, won for her the respect and love of her neighbours; and those who could claim intimacy found in her a rare and beautiful mind.'[27]

Notes

Most of the material in this essay is derived from the private diaries and papers of Florence Vere O'Brien, and is not individually noted here. The notes below therefore refer to other sources.

The 1993 financial equivalents of items included in the text have been converted using consumer price index rates provided by the Central Statistics Office.

1. *History of the O'Briens*, Hon. Donough O'Brien, Batsford, London. 1949. p.234.
2. *Memoir of H. O. Arnold-Forster*, by his wife. Edward Arnold, 1910. pp. 8-10.
3. *Life of the Right Hon. W. E. Forster*, J. Wemyss Reid. Chapman & Hall, 1889. Various.
4. *Florence Arnold-Forster's Irish Journal*, ed. Moody & Hawkins, Clarendon Press, 1988. Various.
5. *History of Lace*, Mrs Bury Palliser, 4th Ed. reprinted Dove, 1984. p. 441.
6. Wife of Robert Vere O'Brien's uncle, Sir Vere de Vere. She was born Mary Lucy Standish. d. 1892.
7. *History of Lace, op. cit.* p. 443 (note) and private papers.
8. *The Arts & Crafts Movement in Ireland*, Larmour. Friar's Bush Press, 1992. pp. 1,2.
9. Lecture given by Alan Cole, reported in *The Munster News and Limerick and Clare Advocate*, Oct 20 1888.
10. *Report on Irish Lace.* Alan Cole. Dept. of Science and Art, 1887. pp. 3, 4.
11. *Ibid.* p. 1.
12. *These my Friends and Forebears*, Grania O'Brien. Ballinakella Press, 1991. p. 171.
13. 4th son of William Smith O'Brien, and first cousin of Robert Vere O'Brien.
14. Alan Cole lecture, *Munster News*, op. cit.
15. Jane was the author's mother. She married Godfrey Hardy in 1928.
16. Columbian Exposition Catalogue, Chicago, 1893.
17. Report on the Belgian Lace Industry, by Mr Pierre Verhaegen. *Irish Times*, 8 Sept. 1902.
18. Royal Dublin Society Industries Exhibition Catalogue, 1903. p. 32.
19. Undated newspaper cuttings.
20. *The Times*, London. 7 Nov. 1904.
21. *Daily Chronicle*, 7 Mar. 1906.
22. *Irish Rural Life and Industry*, Hely's Ltd. p. 134.
23. *Ibid.* Map facing p. 128.
24. Unidentified newspaper cutting, Oct. 1908. Article, 'Ideal Home Industries'.
25. Manuscript Room. Trinity College Dublin, ref. 5038, 5038A.
26. *These my Friends & Forebears. Op. cit.* p. 200.
27. *The Times*, London, 11 July 1936.

Part Three:
Limerick Run (Darned-Net) Lace and Tambour Lace

Instructions and Patterns

(The instructions and patterns in the following pages
are adapted from *Needlecraft No 31 – Limerick Lace*,
published by the Manchester School of Embroidery, c. 1900).

Materials for Run-Lace and Tambour

Fabric:
Fine cotton net. Fine pearl edging to finish off the edges of the finished piece. This may not now be readily available.

 Fig. 1. Pearl Edging.

Thread:
DMC No. 50, sewing cotton: Brilliant D'Alsace No. D. 237.

Needles:
Two sizes are required. A large one, No. 7 for the outline thread and Size 10 Milward embroidery crewel needle for filling or embroidery stitches.

Tracing paper:
Used to draw or transfer the design.

Scissors:
A lacemaker's scissors, while not absolutely necessary is a great advantage.

A frame:
A standard hoop embroidery frame is sufficient for small pieces or the lace can be worked without a frame but it is more difficult to get even results. For larger pieces a proper rectangular embroidery frame is a necessity.

In Ireland, all these materials are generally available at Needlecraft Ltd., 27-28 Dawson St., Dublin 2 (Mr Noel Flavin). However, most good craft supply shops can usually supply the lacemaker's requirements.

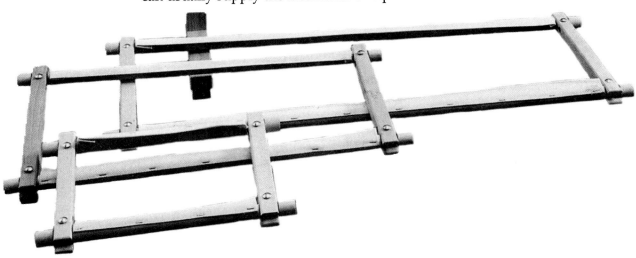

Fig. 2. Modern Frames.

Mounting the net in the frame. Fig. 2

The first process in both Run and Tambour lace is mounting the net in a frame. To do this take the frame apart. You will find a strong piece of webbing tacked along each horizontal bar. The top edge of the net must be tacked closely to one of these, and the lower edge of it to the other. A piece of tape or linen should be carefully sewed along each side edge of the net to bear the strain of lacing, which would tear it. Net is such an elastic material that it is not the easiest thing in the world to mount it. One sighs for a selvedge to guide one in sewing it to the webbing, so that it may be neither gathered in too much, nor yet stretched. A little experience, however, will get over this trouble. When you have both top and bottom sewn to the webbing, you must ascertain if your frame is sufficiently deep to stretch it properly. If you find that your piece of net is too long, you must roll it carefully upon one of the bars till you have the right depth. Screw the nuts in towards the centre of the side bars to enable you to get the top and bottom bars both on them. Then gently screw the nuts out again until the net is evenly and sufficiently stretched. With some very strong thread, lace the tape or linen at either side of the net to the side bars; do not fasten off the thread until both sides are laced and then gently go over the lacing one by one until the net is quite stretched. It must be quite firm and tight all over if you wish to make good lace.

If it has been necessary to roll the net upon one of the bars, you should commence to work at the opposite one, and work towards the rolled portion, finishing as you go along. When you have worked as far as you can, unlace the sides and remove the top and bottom bars, roll up the finished piece of lace, and unroll the unworked piece of net. Replace the bars, and stretch the net as before. By this plan of rolling the work a very long piece of lace can be worked upon a frame of moderate dimensions, provided it is sufficiently broad to take in the width of net properly.

It makes more sense to purchase a medium to large frame rather than a small one. (You can make a small piece on a large frame, but *not* a large piece on a small frame.)

How to make Run Lace

Preparation

Trace the design on to good quality tracing paper. Take a piece of net larger than the design to be worked and sufficiently big to cover the sides of the frame and hold all the net taut.

Tack the net on to the design, working from the centre outwards. Place the net, with design in place in the frame.

Sewing

Take a long piece of your thread which is doubled to outline the design. Place the two ends of the thread together and thread a large needle with them. Then catch the two ends together with your left hand and twist them once round the forefinger of it to form a ring; pass the needle through this and draw the thread close so as to form a tiny knot close below the eye of the needle. Examine the design and choose a starting point carefully, where you can have a good length of outlining without stopping. Take up a bar of net on the needle, and draw it out until only a short length of thread remains, pass the needle through the loop made by the doubling of the thread, draw it close and you have the thread secured in a neat and strong way.

To outline the work you run the needle as nearly as possible over one thread of the net and under the next, along the lines of the design. When you wish to fasten off your thread, make a loop by taking a stitch, pass the needle through the loop, and draw close to form a tiny knot. Do this a second time and then cut the thread close to the last knot. All the threads should be cut off as you go along.

When the outline is entirely worked the design may be removed from the frame. This should be done carefully. It is safer to cut the threads behind the design.

The outline should be filled in after the design is removed. There are two different kinds of stitch generally used for this purpose, viz.: a heavy filling of darning and a light filling of open tent stitch (see figures 3 and 4). After the filling is worked the fancy stitches are added. Both filling and fancy stitches are done with single thread. The fancy stitches are always done in what are called caskets, e.g. a space in the background entirely surrounded by the design. It is never good to crowd in too many stitches for when the background is too much filled with them, the design becomes indistinct and confused.

Pressing

The finished lace should be pressed wrong side uppermost with a warm iron. If the piece is very crushed, a damp cloth may be placed between it and the iron.

FILLINGS AND FANCY STITCHES

In order to make it easy for the readers to learn the method of working the fillings and fancy stitches used in Limerick lace we have produced our illustrations from models worked with coarse cotton upon very coarse net, and in a few of the more

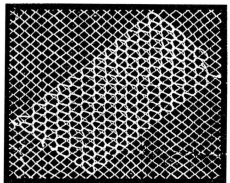

Fig. 3. Heavy Filling.   Fig. 4. Light Filling.

difficult stitches we have shown the direction taken by the working thread upon a piece of thick material which will make it clearer, for the transparency of the net is what makes many stitches appear to be complicated.

There are several matters of which the reader should be reminded to prevent misunderstandings. First, when working fancy stitches you should always pass from one row to the next by overcasting the run outline very neatly. Secondly, a mesh means a hole of the net, square or diamond shaped as you hold it; and a bar means one of the four threads which surround a mesh.

Heavy Filling (Darning) Fig. 3

This darning is done diagonally upon the net. Secure a single thread by knotting it to a bar of net at the edge of some part of the design just outside the running. Pass to the last square of the same diagonal row upon the opposite side of the design; take a stitch just outside the run outline, so as to bring your needle out just one row further on. Again cross to the other side of the design, insert the needle into the same row of squares from which it has just emerged, and bring it out one row further on. Continue thus until you have a thread lying upon each row of squares in the area you wish to fill. These threads must be very carefully and evenly laid; if you miss one, or if you lay one crooked going over two rows of squares, the darning will be uneven and bad. You have now to cross this row by working rows of darning at right angles to these laid stitches.

In doing the darning always pick up a bar of net and miss a thread alternately.

Light Filling. Fig. 4

Light filling, also called 'Tent Stitch', is well illustrated in Fig. 4. Here the effect is obtained by darning your pattern from the top of one bar of net to the diagonal of the line below. In the second row the thread is looped through the line above. This gives a distinct cross-bar effect.

When the stitches are all worked the lace may be removed from the frame and the superfluous net cut away all along the edge of the work. If desired and if it is available, pearl edging sewn all round the outer edges enhances the work and adds to the durability.

FANCY STITCHES FOR THE CASKET

Tent Stitch. Figs. 5 and 6

Tent stitch is the foundation of a great variety of fancy stitches, and it can be worked either horizontally or diagonally upon net. To work it diagonally commence at one end of a row of square meshes, make a stitch across each square, always taking two bars on the needle, until you come to the end of the row. It may

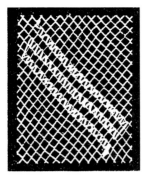

Fig. 5. Diagonal Tent stitch.

Fig. 6. Horizontal Tent stitch.

Fig. 7. Cross stitch (diagonal).

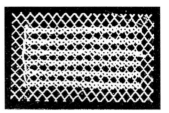

Fig. 8. Cross stitch (horizontal).

be worked either to the right or the left, as may be convenient. To work it horizontally, hold the net so that the meshes appear to be diamond shaped, commence at one side of a space and work across a row, taking a perpendicular stitch behind each place where four bars meet.

Cross Stitch. Figs. 7 and 8

Cross stitch is made by working a row of tent stitch and then returning over it with a second row of the same. It can be worked both horizontally and diagonally.

Net Pattern. Fig. 9

The net pattern at fig. 9 is entirely composed of diagonal rows of tent stitch. It is only one of a series of patterns made upon the same plan. A set of diagonal rows of tent stitch should be worked at intervals, near or far apart as may be desired, across a space; then a second set of rows should be worked at right angles to these, closely following one another. Various check or tartan patterns can be copied by spacing the rows of tent stitch differently.

Net Pattern. Fig. 10

This pattern is composed of a crossbar of diagonal tent stitch so arranged as to leave a space of three meshes and two bars between the rows each way. A satin stitch spot is then worked across the centre mesh of each space, and the thread is carried as unobtrusively as possible from one space to the next.

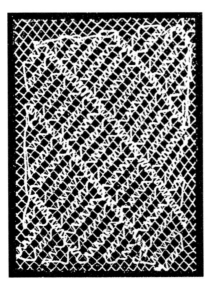

Fig. 9. Net pattern.

Fig. 10. Net pattern.

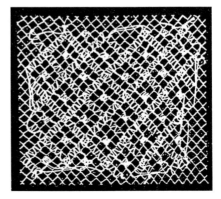

Fig. 11. Net pattern.

Fig. 12. Net pattern.

Net Pattern. Fig. 11

Work diagonal cross stitch in rows leaving spaces of five meshes and four bars between. Cross these with a second series the same distance apart, and at right angles to the first. Work four satin stitch spots from the centre mesh of each space so as to form a small cross.

Net Pattern. Fig. 12

Commence exactly as in fig. 11 but instead of working a cross in the space, work a flower composed of six satin stitch petals radiating from the centre mesh of each space.

Net Pattern. Fig. 13

Work cross stitch as in the two last patterns but make the rows one mesh closer each way. Make a ring by running round the four centre meshes of each space three or four times.

Net Pattern. Fig. 14

Work a series of rows of diagonal cross-stitch leaving five meshes and four bars between. Fill up the spaces between these with rows of crosses. These are formed by working two zig-zag rows of satin stitch.

Fig. 13. Net pattern.

Fig. 14. Net pattern.

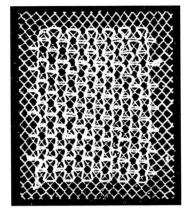
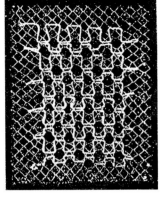

Fig. 15. Net pattern.   Fig. 16. Net pattern.

Net Pattern. Fig. 15

The pattern at Fig. 15 is one which is a great favourite in many different varieties of lace. It is worked horizontally across a space. Commence at the right hand top corner, insert the needle into a mesh, miss the mesh to the left and bring out the needle in the next one. Insert the needle into the mesh immediately below the one missed and bring it out in the next but one to the left. Again insert it where you first brought it out and take a stitch like the first, then another like the second stitch starting from it. Repeat these two till you reach the opposite side of the space. Cross the space again exactly reversing the first row, and let the upper stitches always lie side by side against the lower stitches of the preceding row. If properly worked four stitches should meet in every alternate mesh whether you count them horizontally, vertically, or diagonally.

Net Pattern. Fig. 16

Fig. 16 shows how a very different effect may be produced by piercing every alternate mesh, where the four stitches meet, with a piercer and gently pressing it out, before working the pattern at Fig. 15.

Net Pattern. Fig. 17

The stitch given at Fig. 17 is a most effective one. Work a single row like Fig. 15, then in the return row work a series of fans by making five single satin stitches radiate from the mesh below each lower missed mesh of the preceding row. The third row is like the first row, the top stitches should go from the centre of a fan to the centre of the next. The fourth row is like the second. The top of the centre spike of each fan should go into the centre stitch of each fan of the second row. Repeat these two rows.

Fig. 17. Net pattern.   Showing work on Fig. 17.

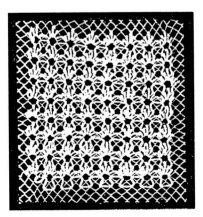
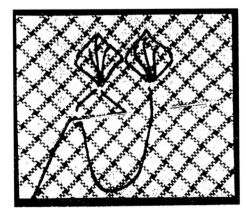

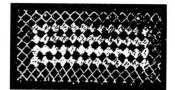

Fig. 18. Net pattern.   Fig. 19. Net pattern.

Net Pattern. Fig. 18

This stitch is worked much like the second row of Fig. 17. Make a fan, then take the thread across a mesh into the next but one and work another fan. Repeat across the whole row. The stitch that is carried from one centre mesh to another will be alternately in front of and behind the missed mesh. In working back make a similar row of fans, but upside down and radiating from the same centres. Where the stitch between the fans went behind in the first row it should come to the front in this one. The next two rows are worked in the same manner, but they are arranged so that the points will come between the fans of the preceeding row.

Net Pattern. Fig. 19

This simple stitch is made by working satin stitch slantwise over each mesh of a horizontal row. When a few rows of it are worked it has something of a chess-board effect.

A Knotted Stitch. Fig. 20

The pretty knotted stitch shown at Fig. 20 is worked much like the well known snail trail so much used in embroidery. It is worked in vertical rows. Insert the needle slantwise from left to right under a mesh and two bars; before drawing out the needle pass the thread from left to right under the point, then draw close. This forms a small knotted stitch which should be repeated all down a line of diamond shaped meshes. In going up the space again for the alternate rows the stitch should be reversed. This makes a pretty pattern for small caskets or for large flower centres.

Net Pattern. Fig. 21

The stitch illustrated here looks much more complicated than it really is; the whole pattern contains but two movements of the needle. Each pattern is worked across

Fig. 20. A knotted stitch.   The making of Fig. 20.   Fig. 21. Net pattern.

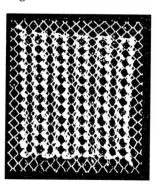
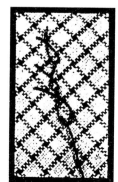
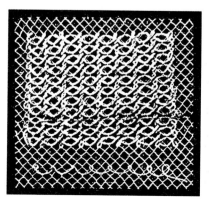

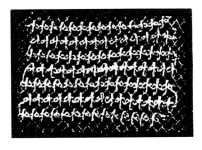

Fig. 22. Net pattern.

The making of Fig. 22.

one horizontal row of diamonds. A half pattern is shown at the lower end of the illustration. Take up the upper point of the first diamond at the left hand end of a row, pointing the needle from right to left, take up the lower point of the next diamond to the right pointing the needle from left to right. Continue these two stitches alternately, taking one into each diamond to the end of the row. This completes the half pattern; you must then work back again in the same manner over the same row of diamonds, but taking the lower point where the upper one was taken before, and the reverse. Repeat these two rows close below, and continue the repetition till the whole space is quite filled.

Net Pattern. Fig. 22

This is a pattern greatly used in Limerick lace. It is rather a puzzling one to copy, but, like many another thing, when once you know how it is done it is extremely easy. Work a solitary horizontal cross stitch upon a diamond beginning at the left side. When making the second half of the cross stitch, bring the needle out below the lower point of the diamond, make a perpendicular stitch by inserting the needle in the mesh above the top of the same diamond, and bring it out where you wish to begin the cross stitch over the next diamond. The effect is very pretty when a casket is filled with rows of this pattern worked close together. A single stitch of it is often used to fill the centre of a small ring.

Net Pattern. Fig. 23

The illustration shows how a string of beads may be effectively represented by outlining them first, and then putting a single stitch of pattern 22 over the centre mesh.

Pierced Holes. Fig. 24

It gives the lace a light and pretty appearance to use a piercer with the centre mesh of a ring pressing it out gently as large as may be, but taking care not to break a thread. When it is pierced the hole should be whipped round to the run outline to keep it from closing up again. These pierced holes are used in various ways, sometimes as a powdering, or perhaps as a small flower centre.

Fig. 23. Net pattern.

Fig. 24. Pierced holes.

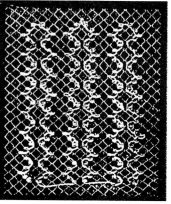

Fig. 25. Net pattern.   Fig. 26. Net pattern.   Fig. 27. Net pattern.

Net Pattern. Fig. 25

This pretty pattern may be worked either horizontally or vertically. The rings are made by running round a diamond twice or three times until the desired thickness is attained; then pass to the diamond next but one, and repeat the running. The rows of rings should be separated by rows of tent stitch, and for a large casket it gives a pretty effect to work the rows of rings turned to right and left alternately, as in the model; for small caskets they may all be turned the same way.

Net Pattern. Fig. 26

This pattern is only suitable for large caskets. It is entirely worked in buttonhole stitch, and may be done in either horizontal or vertical rows. The buttonhole stitches are all taken where four bars meet. Commence at the top of a row and work a buttonhole stitch, pointing the needle directly from right to left. Work two more in the next two meeting places downwards to the right; then two more downwards to the left; work a second buttonhole stitch close beside the last one. Repeat this to the end of the row, when there should be a regular zig-zag line of button-holing. Work a second row back to back with the first, starting so that the zig-zags meet in the same mesh. Repeat these two rows. In the model the patterns are spaced to meet in one mesh at the points. If every alternate pattern is arranged to start one complete mesh lower down, the point of one can fit into the hollow of another. The rows can thus go closer together, and the appearance of the pattern will be quite altered.

Net Pattern. Fig. 27

This pretty pattern does not look as nice as it ought, worked in such coarse cotton, as the passing threads are too conspicuous; but then, that is as they should be for the benefit of learners. Work a cross bar of tent stitch or cross stitch, whichever is preferred, leaving spaces between of five meshes and four bars each way. Commence at the centre mesh of a space and work seven single satin stitches from it into the seven meshes at the outside of half the space, in order; pass where the bars cross to the next space and work half of it in the same way. Continue to the end of the row. Then take a return journey and work the other halves of the same spaces. Fill up all the spaces in the same manner.

Interlaced Ring Pattern. Fig. 28

The interlaced rings in this pattern have a very pretty effect when done with fine thread. Commence with a diamond formed by four meshes together, and darn under the four points of the diamond twice or three times and a quarter, always

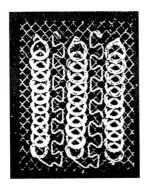
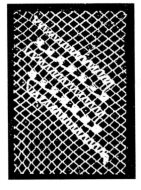

Fig. 28. Interlaced
ring pattern.

Fig. 29. Net pattern.

ending with a side point. Darn the second ring, commencing with the centre of the
first ring which makes the top point of the next diamond. Repeat to the end of the
row. Work a single row of pattern Fig. 15 and a row of interlaced rings alternately.

Net Pattern. Fig. 29

Work a row of diagonal tent stitch, beginning at the left end of it. In the next row
work three satin stitches across a mesh, take a stitch to bring you to the next mesh
but one, work three satin stitches upon it. Continue these spots in every second
mesh to the end of the row. Rows of tent stitch and satin stitch dots should follow
one another alternately. They should be one mesh apart.

Narrow Border Design. Fig. 30

This pretty border has a wild rose design with buds and leaves. The open flowers
are all lightly filled, while the buds and leaves are done with darning. The centres
of the roses are all pierced (see fig. 24), as well as the chain which edges the casket.

Fig. 30. Narrow border in run lace, shown full size.

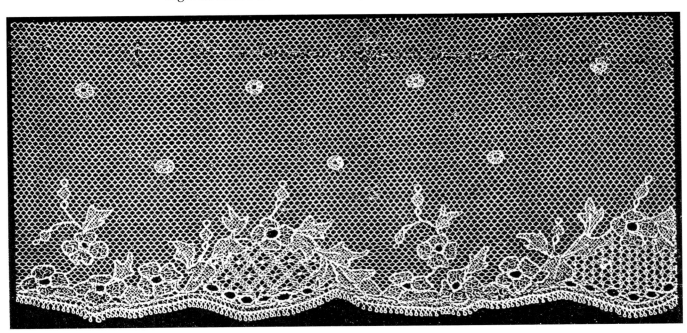

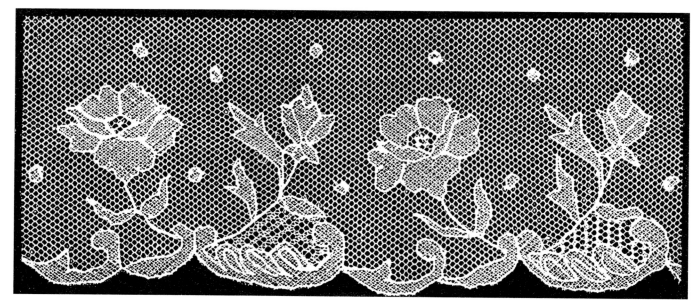

Fig. 31. Medium border in run lace, shown full size.

The fancy stitches are those given at figs. 10, 15 and 22. The spots are formed by outlining a circle with fine cotton, and overcasting it from the centre mesh. These spots are not pierced. The border is finished with pearl edging. This lace would suit for millinery purposes admirably.

Medium Border. Fig. 31
This border is one of a useful width to trim the collar and cuffs of a dress, or to edge a fichu. In the model the design was entirely filled with darning. The centres of the

Fig. 32. Wide border in run lace, shown full size.

Fig. 33. Necktie end in run lace, shown full size.

roses were not filled with it, but rings and satin stitch spots were added. The spots powdered over the design were outlined and darned. The stitches used for filling the casket were those given at figs. 9, 17 and 22.

Wide Border. Fig. 32
The handsome border design given at fig. 32 is entirely filled with darning, but as that is a matter in which the worker can use her own discretion, she may prefer to vary some portions of the design by putting light filling, as, for example, in the small flowers. The centres of these also might sometimes have pierced holes (see fig. 24), or be finished like fig. 23.

Necktie End. Fig. 33
The design in the necktie end is one which is always popular, viz.: the rose, shamrock, and thistle. It is treated in a somewhat conventional style. Both light and heavy fillings are used. Fancy stitches may be selected for the caskets at the worker's pleasure.

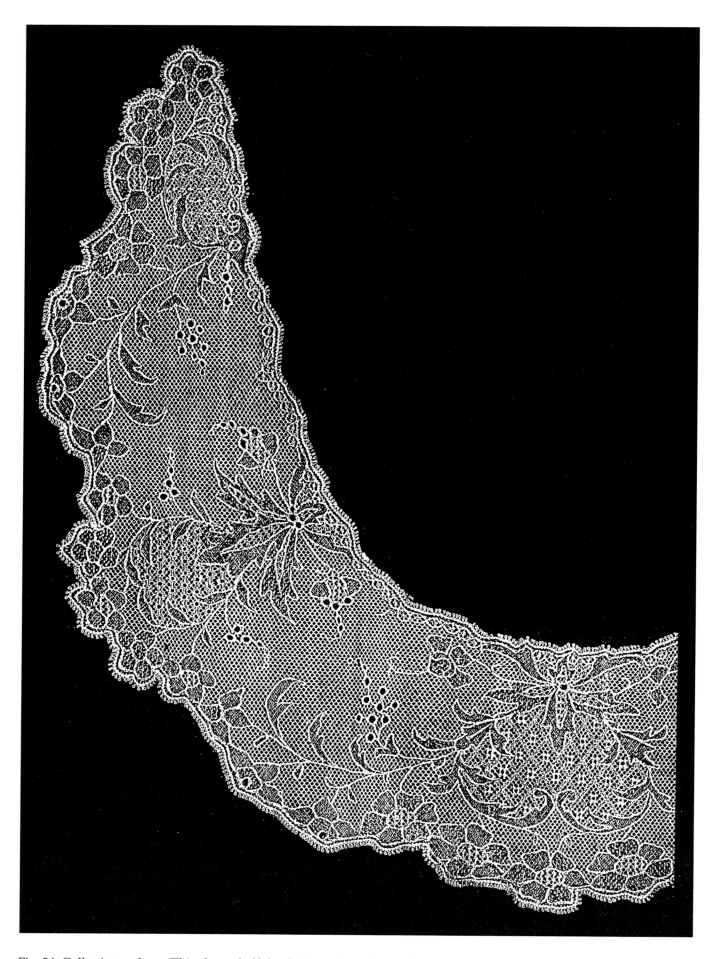

Fig. 34. Collar in run lace. (This shows half the Collar reduced in size).

Fig. 35. Limerick Lace. Section of Berthe. (Original work 4⅛in. wide).

Collar Design. Fig. 34

This lovely collar is one which is not so large as to frighten a timid person who would hesitate to undertake a long or tedious piece of work, yet it is a very pretty one. The bunches of berries made of pierced holes (see Fig. 24) give the lace a very light and pleasant appearance. Some of the flowers are entirely darned, others are done in light filling, while a few have both kinds used in alternate petals. The flower centres are also varied, some being pierced and others filled with fancy stitches. The three most important caskets are filled with stitches given at Figs. 10, 11, and 18. Pearl edging is added last of all as a finish to the collar.

Berthe Design. Fig. 35

The design given at Fig. 35 is a contrast to all the others in the journal, and is arranged from a very old lace design. The filling is entirely done in darning, while light filling is employed as a fancy stitch in some of the smaller caskets. The flower centres are filled with cross-stitch and other net patterns. The stitches used for the larger caskets are to be found at Figs. 15 and 29.

How To Make Tambour Lace

Tambour work using a fine hooked needle is of eastern origin and was known in China, Persia, India and Turkey long before it spread to Europe. It is called tambour from the fact that the frame on which it is worked bears some resemblance to a drum-head or tambourine. On this is stretched a piece of net, the Brussels hexagon variety being the most prized in Ireland. A floss thread or cotton was then drawn by a hooked or tambour needle through the meshes of the net and the design worked from a paper drawing which was placed before the worker. It was not possible to tack the design securely under the net as was done for darned-net. The tambour makers were able to work faster than those making darned net but they had to be more skilled and to some extent their work was freehand. They also had to have the skill to hold the ball of thread under the net with one hand, bring up a loop on their hooked needle, bring up a second loop and then cast off the first loop over the second all the time keeping an eye on the drawing. Some of the trade workers became so expert that when they worked a design a few times they could do small flowers or whole sprays correctly without looking at the design. The outlines of tambour were done with the coarser thread and the fillings with the finer. Sometimes parallel rows of the thick stitch were used to give a heavy outline and to save the workers doing extra lines in finer thread.

In Limerick tambour many 'filling' stitches were also used and these had to be darned in as in run-lace. The same fillings can be used for both types. The workers had names for each stitch like 'chapel window stitch', 'box seed', 'herringbone', 'diamond', 'web', or 'pheasants's eye stitch'. 'Mrs O'Brien's stitch' used by Kinsale workers was another surviving name but we do not know to which filling stitch the name was applied.

Most Limerick lace was finished with a pearl edging which was sewn on by hand when the main work was completed. Some purists thought the pearl edging

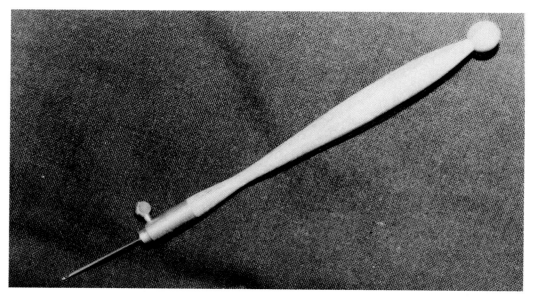

Fig. 36. Modern Tambour Needle. Photo: D. Rowe.

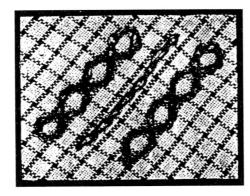

Fig. 37. Tambour net pattern.

Fig. 38. Tambour net pattern.

should never be used and that the work should be finished with invisible button-holing, a more expensive process.

Tambour Net Pattern. Fig. 37

The pattern illustrated at Fig. 37 is worked diagonally upon the net. The tambour stitch is taken across the top of the first square, slantwise down the second, across the bottom of the third, and slantwise up the fourth. Repeat this all along the row, and take a return journey in reverse order. A single straight line of tambour alternating with a curved one makes a very pretty pattern.

Tambour Net Pattern. Fig. 38

This effective pattern is also worked diagonally in rows backwards and forwards. First stitch, across two bars and one mesh. Second stitch, slantwise, going one bar back and two bars and one mesh down. Third stitch, across two bars and one mesh. Fourth stitch, one bar back and two bars and one mesh up. Repeat these four stitches. In every following row let the upper stitches lie along the lower stitches of each preceding row.

Tambour Net Pattern. Fig. 39

This pattern is worked in vertical lines up and down. The spots are made round every alternate diamond by working tambour stitch across the left, lower, right, and top corners in order, and then into the centre; work straight across the next diamond, and repeat this to the end of the row.

Tambour Net Pattern. Fig. 40

This pattern is worked across a diagonal row of meshes. The stitches are taken side about into every mesh, making a close zig-zag. It has something the effect of cross-

Fig. 39. Tambour net pattern.

Fig. 40. Tambour net pattern.

Fig. 41. Tambour lace scarf (original work 10in. wide).

Fig. 42. Border in tambour lace, shown full width.

stitch to a casual observer, and may be used exactly as the latter is used in run lace. It makes, for example, cross-bar patterns of various kinds, sometimes with tabour-stitch spots in the centres of the spaces.

Tambour Lace Scarf. Fig. 41

This handsome tambour lace scarf is outlined with the No. 50 cotton, and filled with loosely worked tambour stitch in the same cotton. The caskets are filled with the three net patterns given at Figs. 37, 38 and 39. Fig. 39 is used for the centres of the three large daisies, but in these it is worked closely with no rows of net meshes between. A solid spot of tambour stitch is worked in each centre of the daisy chain border as well as in many of the berries and trefoils. Two solid spots form the centres of the roses. The scarf is finished with pearl edging.

Border In Tambour Lace. Fig. 42

The border illustrated at Fig. 42 is a graceful design of periwinkle flowers. The outlines, midribs and veinings are all worked in the No. 50 thread, and the filling is done in loosely worked tambour stitch. Fancy tambour patterns fill the caskets between the scalloped border and the floral design.

Advertisement about 1900.

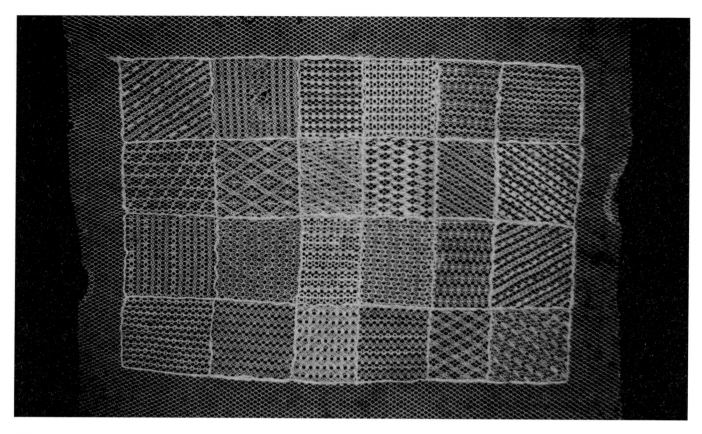

Filling stitches used in Limerick Lace School c. 1900. Rowe collection. Photo: Colin Smyth.

The threads now being suggested are the finest that are currently available. Those threads used in the original instructions (Nos. 120 and 250), were finer, but they are no longer readily available.

Bibliographical Note

First hand information comes from interviews with Sister Mary de Lourdes who had been in charge of the lace-room at Benada Abbey in Sligo in 1935; from interviews with the nuns in the Mercy Convent Kinsale, the Good Shepherd Convent in Limerick and the Presentation Convent in Cahirciveen, Co. Kerry. We are grateful to the Convents who provided information from their Annals, especially to the Good Shepherd Convent in Limerick.

Previously unpublished material comes from the papers of Mrs Vere O'Brien, and from information given by Miss D. Stewart, a great grand-daughter of Mrs Mary Mills (who came to Limerick with Courtaulds in the 1840s), to Veronica Rowe.

Books

Aberdeen, Lord and Lady. *We Twa*. Glasgow: William Collins, 1925.

Souvenir Album from the Aberdeen's staff 1905-1915. Dublin, n.d.

Arnold-Forster, Mrs H. O. *Memoir of H. O. Arnold-Forster*, London: Edward Arnold, 1910.

Blackburn, Helen. *A Handy Book of Reference for Irish Women*. Pub. for the Irish Exhibition, Olympia. London, 1888.

Bowe, Nicola Gordon. *The Dublin Arts and Crafts Movement 1885-1930*, Dublin: Bowe, 1985.

Boyle, Elizabeth. *The Irish Flowerers*. Belfast, 1971.

Brenan, James. *Art Instruction in Ireland. Ireland Industrial & Agricultural*, Dublin: Browne & Nolan, 1902.

Cole, Alan. *Irish Lace Report*, Department of Science & Art, London, 1887.

A.S.C. (Alan S. Cole). *A Renascence of the Irish Art of Lace-making*. London: Chapman & Hall, 1888, facsimile reprint, Belfast: Ulster Folk & Transport Museum, 1988.

Cole, Alan. *Lace Making in Ireland*, London: Department of Science & Art, 1890.

Cole, Alan S. *Report upon visits to Irish lacemaking and embroidery schools*. 1897. London. 1898.

Coyne William P., ed. *Ireland Industrial and Agricultural*. Dublin, Cork & Belfast: Department of Agriculture and Technical Instruction for Ireland, Browne & Nolan 1902.

de Dillmont, Therese. *Encyclopedie des Ouvrages de Dames*. Dornach, Alsace ante 1898. Translated as *The Complete Encyclopedia of Needlework*.

Dudding, Jean. *Coggeshall Tambour Lace*, Dudding, 1988.

Dudding, Jean 'Creating Coggeshall Lace', Dudding 1988.

Dunlevy, Mattead: *Dress in Ireland*. London: Batsford, 1989.

Earnshaw, Pat: *Limerick Run Laces, an introduction*. Guildford: Gorse Publications, 1992.

Feldman, Annette. *Handmade Lace and Patterns*. New York: Harper & Row, 1975.

Hall, Mr and Mrs Samuel. *Ireland. Its scenery and character*. Vol. 1. Tour taken 1838 and 1840. London: Hall, Virtue & Co., 1841.

Hall, Mr and Mrs Samuel. *Handbooks for Ireland. The South and Killarney*. London:

Hall, Virtue & Co., 1853.

Hall, Mr and Mrs S.C., *Ireland, its Scenery and Character*. London: Hall, Virtue & Co., 1855.

Kane, Robert. *The Industrial Resources of Ireland*. Dublin: Hodges & Smith, 1844.

Larmour, Paul. *Arts & Crafts Movement in Ireland*, Dublin: Friar's Bush Press, 1992.

Levey, Santina. *Laces and History*, London: Victoria & Albert Museum, 1983.

Lewis, Samuel. *Topographical Dictionary*. London: S. Lewis, 1837.

Lindsey, Ben. *Limerick Lace. Its Origin and History*, Dublin, 1886.

Longfield, Ada K. *Guide to the Collection of Lace*. Dublin National Museum of Ireland, 1970.

Longfield, Ada K. *Irish Lace*, Dublin: Eason & Sons, 1978.

Longfield, Ada K. *Catalogue to the Collection of Lace*, Dublin: National Museum of Ireland, N.D.

W.T.M-F. (W.T. Macartney-Filgate). *Irish Rural Life and Industry*. Dublin, 1907.

Marmion, Anthony. *The Ancient & Modern History of the Maritime Ports of Ireland*. London: Marmion, 4th Ed., 1860.

Martin, R. M. 'The Manufacture of Lace & Crochet in Ireland', *Irish Rural Life & Industry*, Dublin: Hely's Ltd, 1907.

Meredith, Mrs, née Twamley. *The Lacemakers*. London 1865.

O'Brien, Grania R. *These my Friends and Forebears*, Whitegate, Co. Clare: Ballinakella Press, 1991.

O'Brien, Mrs Vere, 'The Limerick Lace Industry', *Irish Homestead Special*. Dublin, 1897.

Pallisser, Mrs Bury. *History of Lace,* ed. and extended by M. Jourdain and Alice Dryden. London 1976. 4th Ed. reprint, Dove, 1984.

Petheridge, Janette. '*A Manual of Lace*'. London: Cassell, 1947.

Pond, Gabrielle. *An Introduction to Lace*. London: Garnstone Press, 1973.

Reid, J. Wemyss. *Life of the Rt. Hon. W. E. Forster*, London: Chapman & Hall, 1889.

Robinson, Sir Henry, Bart., K.C.B., *Memories Wise and Otherwise*. London, Toronto and Melbourne: Cassell, 1923.

Rolleston, T. W. ed. *Journal and proceedings of the Arts and Crafts Society of Ireland*. Dublin, 1901.

Simeon, Margaret. *The History of Lace*. London: Stainer & Bell, 1978.

Taylor, Fanny. *Irish Homes and Irish Hearts*. London: Longmans, Green & Co., 1867.

Victorian History of the County of Essex, Volume 2. Essex Record Office, 1907.

Wardle, Patricia. *Victorian Lace*. London: Herbert Jenkins, 1968.

Warwick, M. & D. *Eminent Victorians, The Forsters of Burley-in-Wharfedale*, Burley in Wharfedale, Local History Group Publications, 1994.

Periodicals and Reports

Digest of Evidence given to the Congested Districts Board.

Dublin Historical Record 1984/5. (Records of the College of Art, Dublin) edited by Professor Turpin.

Extract from an untitled and undated extract of a lace article on Limerick obtained from Sister Marguerite, Good Shepherd Convent, Limerick, in 1984.

Journal & Proceedings of the Arts & Crafts Society of Ireland, Vol. 1, No. 3, 1901.

Limerick City and County Directory. Limerick: Wm. Bassett, 1881.

Needlecraft Practical Journal No. 31. Limerick Lace, Run and Tambour. Manchester, c. 1900.

New Ireland Review, Sept. 1894 to Feb. 1895: Monthly. Fallon & Co., 1894.

Obituary Charles Walker from *Limerick Chronicle* 4 November 1943, p. 2.

Records of the Congested Districts Board. (1893-1923). Stationery Office. Dublin: Alex Thorn.

Reports of Exhibitions, including Dublin; Crystal Palace London, Cork, 1883; Paris,

1867; Chicago, 1893.

Robinson, Mabel. *'Irish Lace'. Art Journal* 1887.

Sixth Series Chambers Journal June 1899. Article by Mary Gorges. *The Irish Home Industries.* London & Edinburgh, p. 375.

Slainte: Journal of the Women's National Health Association of Ireland. ed. Countess of Aberdeen. Dublin. 1909-1911.

Scrapbook owned by Anita Puigcerver-Rumbold compiled by her grand-aunt Mrs May Nugent Popoff.

The Lady of the House, article 15 September 1891.

Catalogues

Art Industries Exhibition, Royal Dublin Society, 1903.

Royal Irish Industries Sale Programme, Manchester, 1907.

Royal Irish Industries Sale Programme, Brighton, 1910.